Christmas
DOUGHCRAFTS

Dedicated to my dear friend, Janet

Christmas DOUGHCRAFTS

ELISABETH BANG

CASSELL

A CASSELL BOOK

First published 1995

by Cassell

Wellington House

125 Strand

London

WC2R 0BB

Copyright © Elisabeth Bang 1995

Design by Maggie Aldred and Tony Paine

Photography by Paul Bricknell

Distributed in the United States

by Sterling Publishing Co., Inc.

387 Park Avenue South

New York

New York 10016-8810

Distributed in Australia

by Capricorn Link (Australia) Pty Ltd

2/13 Carrington Road

Castle Hill

NSW 2154

British Library Cataloguing-in-Publication Data

A catalogue record for this book is available from the British Library

ISBN 0-304-34395-1

Typeset by Litho Link Ltd., Welshpool, Powys, Wales.

Printed in Portugal by Printer Portuguesa

Contents

Introduction

Combining salt and flour is an ancient practice. As far back as biblical times the two ingredients were in use together. In the 1800s American sailors would take the dough cakes on their voyages, giving rise to the nickname 'Dough boys'. Today, in Middle Eastern countries, bread and salt is used to seal an oath. Salt dough has been a worldwide art form for centuries. Delightful interpretations of the craft are found in such countries as sunny Mexico and the winter chills of Scandinavia.

In Europe, it is an age-old tradition to make decorations and gifts from dough to celebrate the Christmas festival. The possibilities of this medium are endless, its versatility giving ample scope to both the

complete beginner and the skilled craftsperson. Salt dough is very tactile by nature. Working with it can be both therapeutic and rewarding. It is also relatively cheap, salt and flour being the main ingredients. Scour your local charity shops for ideas and equipment; there are many useful items and shapes to be found in them, such as candle holders, stainless steel dishes and suchlike to use as moulds. This book is full of original and unusual ideas to copy, from the traditional nativity figures, Christmas decorations and the ever-popular gingerbread house, to useful gifts such as the working clock face, or

jewellery ideas. With easy to follow, step-by-step instructions and beautiful colour photography, you will not only be able to master the craft but also develop your own ideas.

Once you take up the challenge you are sure to become addicted to this charming craft, to such an extent that your ovens will be brimming over with ideas. Remember you still have to cook the Christmas dinner! You could make some items for the school fête or Christmas bazaar.

Keep your ideas simple at first, and experiment with cookie cutters to get the feel of the dough. As you become more adventurous, try your hand at three-dimensional shapes. The dough is moulded or rolled; experiment with your kitchen tools to achieve different textures on the surface. For example, dough forced through a garlic press will produce long thin strips ideal for hair. Imprint the dough with lace, wire mesh, sculpted metal, buttons, or anything suitable from the work box or sewing basket. Add interesting items to the dry dough, such as dried flowers, seeds or beads. Colour the dough with spices, food colours or paint. Picture frame gilt rubbed on to the model before varnishing gives a dramatic effect.

Above all, the main aim of this book is to show what fun you can have with the craft of salt dough. Good luck with your projects, and have a happy and productive Christmas!

CHAPTER ONE

Getting Started

Inspiration

There is a range of classic and original ideas suitable for the dough enthusiast and the newcomer alike in this book. Many sources of inspiration lend themselves to doughcraft; look to the local library, magazines, greeting cards, Christmas catalogues and nature for ideas.

Equipment

First, have all your equipment ready for use. There is nothing worse than delving into kitchen drawers with flour-covered hands.

You will already have most of the items needed for creating our delightful ideas in your kitchen. The following provides a list of helpful items with their uses.

Bamboo skewers/cocktail sticks: for supporting the dough model, imprinting patterns and making holes.

Cake spatula/fish slice: for easing and lifting dough off the work surface and on to the baking sheet.

Compass: for drawing perfect circles on card.

Cookie cutters: hardware shops stock a vast range, from festive Christmas shapes to popular circular and heart shapes. These make excellent tree decorations.

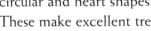

★ ★ ★ ★ ★ ★ ★ ★ ★ ★ ★

10

Fork: for making imprints around the edge of dough or rows of dots.

Garlic press: produces long thin strands of dough. Hole sizes may vary from manufacturer to manufacturer. Ideal for making strands of hair, beards, animal fur, foliage, grass or waves.

Icing cutters: these are smaller than cookie cutters, and so are perfect for cutting delicate shapes. There are many different shapes to choose, such as holly, ivy, flowers and bells.

Icing nozzles: for imprinting patterns on dough. Wide-ended nozzles make circles, suitable for flat beads. Star-shaped nozzles make patterns.

Kitchen knife: for cutting and shaping dough.

Pastry brush: for brushing dough with water to secure one piece to another; also for brushing dough with egg glaze before the browning process.

Rolling pin: rolling dough to required even thickness, such as for making plaques.

Scissors: for trimming and snipping dough into points; see, for example, the owl's feathers on page 61.

Sieve/strainer: produces thin strands of dough depending on the gauge of the mesh. Similar uses as the garlic press, but more suitable for use on small-scale models of up to 4 in (10 cm) in height.

Table-/dessertspoon: for use as moulds; for example, the love spoons.

Other useful items: cookie trays and racks, flan rings, baking parchment, cooking foil, string, greaseproof paper, card, paintbrushes of assorted sizes, watercolour/poster paints, watercolour varnish, comb, spirit for cleaning brushes, ruler.

★ ★ ★ ★ ★ ★ ★ ★ ★ ★ ★ ★ ★

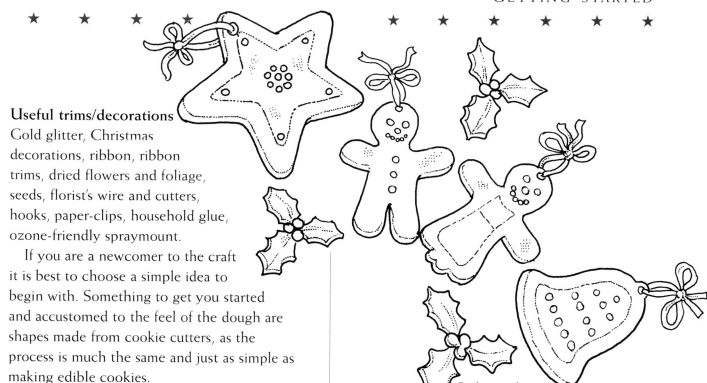

Cookie cut shapes

Useful trims/decorations

Gold glitter, Christmas decorations, ribbon, ribbon trims, dried flowers and foliage, seeds, florist's wire and cutters, hooks, paper-clips, household glue, ozone-friendly spraymount.

If you are a newcomer to the craft it is best to choose a simple idea to begin with. Something to get you started and accustomed to the feel of the dough are shapes made from cookie cutters, as the process is much the same and just as simple as making edible cookies.

Make sure that your work-room is not too hot and, if using a work top, check that the lighting is not situated directly over the dough. Warm conditions, whether from lights, central heating or your own body heat, can dry out the dough. Have a damp cloth nearby to cover dough when not in use.

Dough Recipes

There are varying schools of thought about which are the best recipes for doughcrafts. The more experienced you become, the more you may develop your own quantities and preferences, so keep a note of what you have used. Some projects in this book are made using the different recipes and showing the results you will achieve from them. Standard all-purpose flour and cooking salt are ideal for stock recipes, while rye flour gives a darker, rustic appearance to the dough. The following recipes provide a good base from which to work. Use a straight-sided mug to measure the amounts of flour, salt and water for the recipes.

Basic dough

This recipe is ideal for most samples in this book, and perfect for children to work with. It is possible to add up to one dessertspoon of vegetable oil to the basic recipe for a smoother, more pliable mixture, or one tablespoon of wallpaper paste for an elastic dough. Combine the wallpaper flakes or powder with water before adding to the dough, or mix with the dry ingredients.

11

Recipe for basic dough

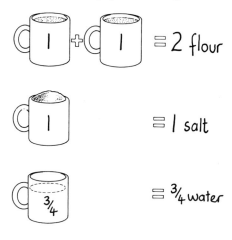

★ ★ ★ ★ ★ ★ ★ ★ ★ ★ ★ ★ ★ ★ ★

Firm dough

By increasing the salt and reducing the water content, the texture becomes drier. This recipe is excellent where you require different textures or the dough has to support itself, as in free-standing figures.

Fine dough

For intricate work such as in jewellery or delicate petals, add a mug of potato flour to the basic recipe.

Recipe for firm dough

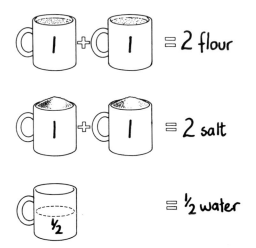

$$\boxed{I} + \boxed{I} \equiv 2 \text{ flour}$$

$$\boxed{I} + \boxed{I} \equiv 2 \text{ salt}$$

$$\boxed{\tfrac{1}{2}} \equiv \tfrac{1}{2} \text{ water}$$

Wallpaper adhesives may contain fungicides; do not let young children use dough containing this substance, as they may eat it or put dough-covered fingers into their mouths. If you are using a wooden rolling pin keep one specifically for your dough work to prevent any fungicide being absorbed by the wood.

Preparing the basic dough

Measure the quantities of salt and flour into a large mixing bowl. Stir the dry ingredients with a spoon, make a well in the centre and gradually add enough tepid water to form a pliable dough with your hands. Empty half of the mixture on to your work surface and keep the remainder covered. The dough is now ready for kneading.

Knead the dough as you would for bread or pastry on a flour-covered work top. Pull it towards you with your fingers and knuckles and push down with the part of your palms closest to your wrists. The dough must be kept as cool as possible, so do not use the middle of your palms. After 10 minutes the dough should be workable, producing a pliable consistency. Hold the bulk of dough downwards in your hand to test its elasticity. If it drops quickly it is too moist, so add some flour and knead it again. Work remaining mixture as above. (It is possible to mix dough in a food processor, follow the manufacturer's instructions for bread making.) Let the prepared dough relax for 30 minutes in a plastic bag or container, after which the dough is ready for use. You can store your dough for up to two days in sealed plastic containers. However, to be certain of best results, freshly made dough is preferable. Make enough dough for your project; the basic recipe makes a 4 in (10 cm) figure, or the Santa plaque as shown here (see page 111 for fuller instructions).

12

★ ★ ★ ★ ★ ★ ★ ★ ★ ★ ★ ★ ★ ★ ★

The mixing method is the same for other recipes. Combine additional ingredients, such as cooking oil, with the dry ingredients and the water. Wallpaper adhesive can be added as powder or flakes, or as a paste, to the dry ingredients.

If you have sensitive skin, wear fine surgical gloves to prevent your skin drying out from contact with the salt.

Colouring dough

You will achieve a rustic appearance by adding rye flour to the basic dough recipe. As it is heavier than all-purpose flour it is better to combine the two. It takes longer to dry out, so air-dry your model before finishing in the oven. The length of time required will depend on its thickness.

Recipe for coloured dough

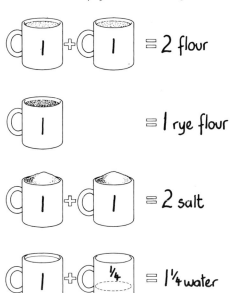

$$1 + 1 = 2 \text{ flour}$$

$$1 = 1 \text{ rye flour}$$

$$1 + 1 = 2 \text{ salt}$$

$$1 + \tfrac{1}{4} = 1\tfrac{1}{4} \text{ water}$$

13

Other colouring agents such as food colours, ground spices, cocoa and coffee can be added to the basic recipe. For smaller quantities of different colours, divide the dough into little balls and colour each with your chosen colouring. Flatten the ball, indent the centre, add the colour and wrap the dough around it, kneading in the colour thoroughly. To achieve a marbled or patterned effect to the dough, knead different food colours together. Cross-sections of dough reveal unusual patterns. Painting hardened dough is the easiest way to colour your model (see Chapter 4 on painting for the technique). You can also colour your model after cooking with artist's gold paste.

Dough paste

Dough paste is made from a ball of dough mixed in a cup with water to a creamy consistency. This is used for bonding hardened dough together.

★ ★ ★ ★ ★ ★ ★ ★ ★ ★ ★ ★ ★ ★ ★

CHAPTER TWO

Modelling Techniques

Make your model either on a floured work top, directly on to a lightly oiled baking tray to prevent the dough from sticking, or over a sheet of baking parchment. Each method has advantages and disadvantages. A floured work top allows the design to grow in size as you model it, but lifting the shape on to a baking tray may damage it. Working directly on a baking tray limits the size of your model, but gives an even base to the model suitable for plaques.

A parchment lining enables the model to be moved easily, but can cause wrinkles on the underside. You may wish to work on aluminium foil, but it may stick to the model, and is only recommended for protecting your work from burning or to act as a support during the drying process.

Cutting shapes from sheet of dough

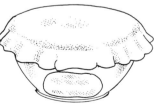

Make small holes in the separate shapes

Cut shapes

Start with something easy, such as tree decorations stamped out with shaped cookie cutters. Form half the basic recipe into a ball, roll the dough to a thickness of ¼ in (6 mm) and check for cracks in the dough. Press the cutters into the dough to release the shape. If using different shaped cutters, lay each one on top of

★ ★ ★ ★ ★

Plaques and flat sheets of dough

The best recipe to use is the basic one combined with wallpaper glue (see page 11), as it enables you to roll the dough with ease. The glue in the mixture gives greater extension when rolled thin. The clock face on page 68 is a good example of this method.

Plaques and flat sheets of dough form the foundations for many designs. You can paint the flat area, or add dough shapes to give further dimensions. Additional shapes can be added before or after drying in the oven. Bond the uncooked dough with water, and the hardened dough with dough paste.

Bas-relief

As with the above plaques and sheets, the dough is modelled on to a hardened base. After drying attach shapes with dough paste and then dry the finished model. The following bases are ideal for fixing dough shapes on top: plywood or cut wood (stained or painted), cork mats, woven straw mats, ceramic tiles.

Rolled dough

Rolling dough into long tubular shapes is a technique suitable for young children, and is no doubt something that many adults remember doing with plasticine as children! The tube shape is extremely versatile, and forms the base of many ideas in this book, from heart shapes and garlands to vertical shapes.

the rolled dough to gauge the best cutting layout and usage of the dough. Using a fish slice, lift the shapes on to a cookie tray lined with baking parchment. Make a hole in the top of each shape for a hanging thread with the blunt end of a bamboo skewer.

Decorate the cut shapes of dough with any of the following methods. Paint a pattern on the model when it is cooked, stick on seeds, or make three-dimensional decorations with dough shapes stuck on the front. To join one piece of dough to another moisten both sections with water which helps the dough to bond during drying. Create your own templates for cutting out shapes from patchwork plastic. This is ideal, as it has a pre-marked grid to help trace designs and is washable, so you can use it repeatedly.

Other ideas in this book accompany their own specific modelling methods. These will help you to develop your own thoughts and skills.

15

Splay fingers to roll dough backwards and forwards

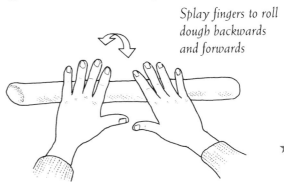

Twisted tubes

Angle ends

Join ends

16

your palms flat on the dough and repeat the rolling process from the centre to the outer edges. Keep the pressure of your hands even so that the tube maintains its circumference. Uneven rolling will cause the dough to taper and split.

Make the second tube to the same dimensions as the first, repeating the rolling technique. Moisten the centre of one tube with water and lay the other tube on top to form a cross shape. Take an end in each hand and gently twist the pieces over from the middle outwards. Angle one end upwards and its opposite end downwards with a sharp knife and squeeze the ends of the dough together. Moisten the angled ends with water before pressing them over each other to close a ring.

Twisted roll

This is the foundation for the twisted dough garland. Make it small for use as a napkin ring, bottle decoration, etc., and large for a garland, horseshoe or heart shape; simply vary the circumference of the tubes.

Squeeze a ball of dough into a thick oblong tube. Place your fingertips on the top edge of the dough and gently roll the dough backwards and forwards towards and away from you. Lay

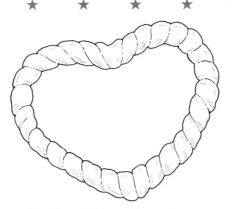

Dented circle forming heart shape

Heart shape in twisted dough

A twisted dough garland heart can be shaped by forming the dough ring into a heart shape on the baking tray.

Braided dough

Plait together three tubes of equal width and length to create a solid braid. This joined in a ring is ideal for garlands, wreaths and circular table decorations. Experiment with the following to embellish the braided dough: dried flowers, dough fruit, dough holly and ivy, feathers, silk flowers, pasta shapes, seeds.

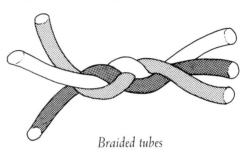

Braided tubes

Glue on additional features that may be affected by the oven temperatures after the drying process.

Hang garlands by tying ribbon around the plaited dough at the top, or by inserting a paper-clip (see page 34).

17

Twisted braid-shaped dough

You can create braids from dough twisted lengthwise; decorate them with dough shapes, dried flowers or seeds. If the braid is for hanging, remember to make a hole at the top or insert a paper-clip for the hanging loop. To make a self-hanging loop, fold a long tube of dough in half and then twist it together.

Self-made hanging loop

CHAPTER THREE

Figures

Flat modelled figures
Approximate height 9 in (23 cm)

This method is used for shaping the figures on hanging plaques, or for figures to be added to a flat base such as the chef on page 7 and choir boys illustrated here.

Beginning with the head, take enough dough to make a ball about 1½ in (4 cm) in diameter. Roll the ball between your palms. Flatten the dough into a disc, grading from ¼ in (6 mm) at the edge to ½ in (12 mm) in the centre and ¼ in (6 mm) at the other edge. Insert a 1½ in (4 cm) length of cocktail stick into the lower edge of the disc, pressing dough around it to secure in position.

To make the body, roll a tube of dough into an oblong 4 in (10 cm) x 2 in (5 cm), and flatten the length. For further shapes add extra balls of dough to the appropriate area. By moulding dough in the middle of the body you can create a fat stomach; for an adult female model, small balls of dough of equal size can be added for breasts. Half way up the body, squeeze the dough at the sides to form the waist, and shape the tube at the top to fashion the neck.

To join the head to the body, moisten the top edge of the body piece. Press the cocktail stick with the head attached to it down on to the top of the body section, taking care that the stick does not penetrate the surface.

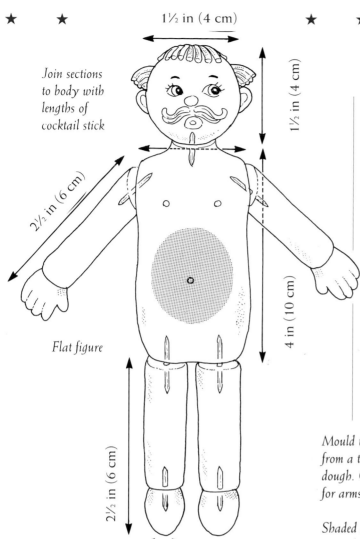

Join sections to body with lengths of cocktail stick

1½ in (4 cm)

1½ in (4 cm)

2½ in (6 cm)

4 in (10 cm)

Flat figure

2½ in (6 cm)

¾ in (2 cm)

Fashion the hands and feet from dough balls of equal size joined at the bottom of the arm and leg tubes with cocktail sticks or water. You can leave the arms and legs straight or as if in action, for example, holding a basket, ice skating, etc., by notching at the joints and bending limbs into appropriate positions.

The easiest way to make hair for the figure is by pressing dough through a garlic press. Add hair after the clothing, or it will get in the way of collar and neckline detail. Moisten the top of the head, arrange the hair so that it falls each side of the face and add short lengths of dough across the forehead to form a fringe.

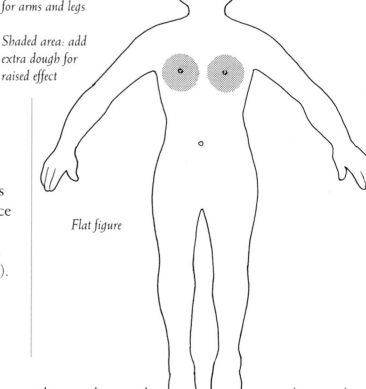

Mould the body from a tube of dough. Cut into it for arms and legs

Shaded area: add extra dough for raised effect

Flat figure

19

Roll two tubes measuring 2½ in (6 cm) x ¾ in (2 cm) for the legs. Insert a ¾ in (2 cm) length of cocktail stick into each of the tubes at the top. Moisten the base of the body piece and press the legs' sticks into the dough.

Make arms as for the legs from two dough tubes measuring 1½ in (4 cm) x ½ in (12 mm). Angle the top edge of each by cutting the dough away with a sharp knife. Dampen the cut edge and press on to the body piece at the shoulders.

Tubby figures

It is possible to make a figure with the body, arms and legs shaped from one piece of dough. Divide the dough into sections with a knife and shape the limbs and body with your fingers and thumbs. Attach the head to the body with a cocktail stick. For example, you can make Santa's little helpers by using this method.

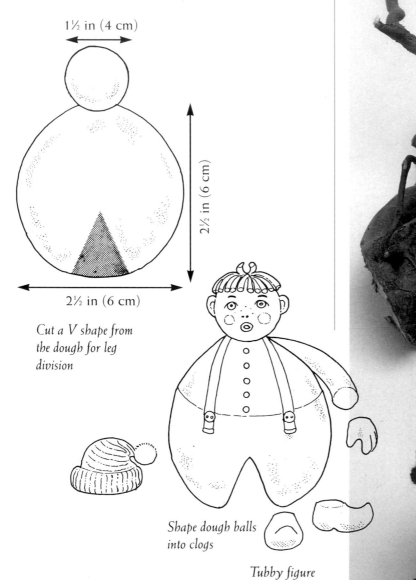

1½ in (4 cm)

2½ in (6 cm)

2½ in (6 cm)

Cut a V shape from the dough for leg division

Shape dough balls into clogs

Tubby figure

★ ★ ★ ★ ★ ★ ★ ★ ★ ★ ★ ★ ★ ★ ★

FREE-STANDING FIGURES

There are several ways in which free-standing dough figures can be supported: with their own hollow base, or modelled on their own support vehicle of pre-dried dough.

Hollow based figures

Cut out an 8 in (20 cm) circle from card: an old cereal box is ideal for this purpose. Snip up to the centre of the card, overlap the cut edges and staple them together. Trim the point and the base so that it will stand evenly. Roll a circle of dough to ¼ in (6 mm) thick and ½ in (12 mm) larger than the circumference of the card. Slit up to the centre of the dough circle with a knife. Wrap the dough circle around the card cone, moisten the overlapping edges and fasten by pressing together. Cut the excess dough from the base. The cone can be dried, or worked while soft.
Roll a ball of dough for the head and squeeze the base between index finger and thumb to form the neck section. Dampen the

Dress

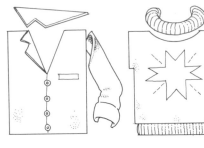

Pyjamas

Jumper

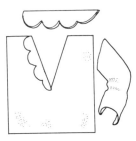

Nightdress

Chef's top

Cape

Baby face, modelled nose and mouth

Girl, painted face

Boy with wire glasses

Card mould: slash circle, join with adhesive tape

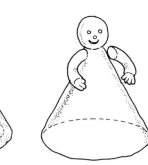

Teenager with braids

Woman

Man, beard, modelled nose

★ ★ ★ ★ ★ ★ ★ ★ ★ ★ ★ ★ ★ ★ ★

★ ★ ★ ★ ★ ★ ★ ★ ★ ★ ★ ★ ★ ★ ★ ★

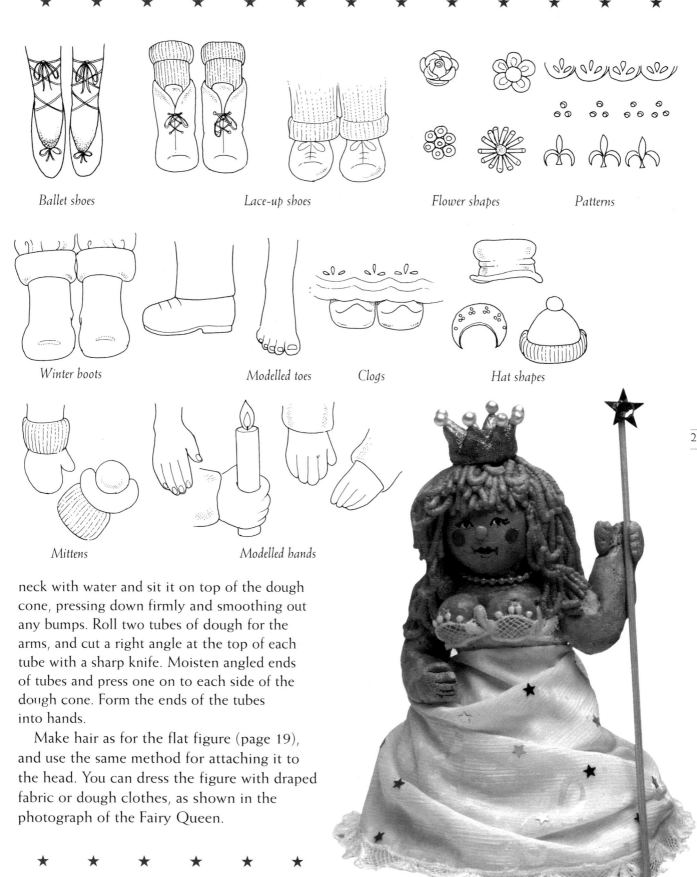

Ballet shoes   *Lace-up shoes*   *Flower shapes*   *Patterns*

Winter boots   *Modelled toes*   *Clogs*   *Hat shapes*

Mittens   *Modelled hands*

neck with water and sit it on top of the dough
cone, pressing down firmly and smoothing out
any bumps. Roll two tubes of dough for the
arms, and cut a right angle at the top of each
tube with a sharp knife. Moisten angled ends
of tubes and press one on to each side of the
dough cone. Form the ends of the tubes
into hands.

Make hair as for the flat figure (page 19),
and use the same method for attaching it to
the head. You can dress the figure with draped
fabric or dough clothes, as shown in the
photograph of the Fairy Queen.

★ ★ ★ ★ ★ ★ ★

★ ★ ★ ★ ★ ★ ★ ★ ★ ★ ★ ★ ★ ★

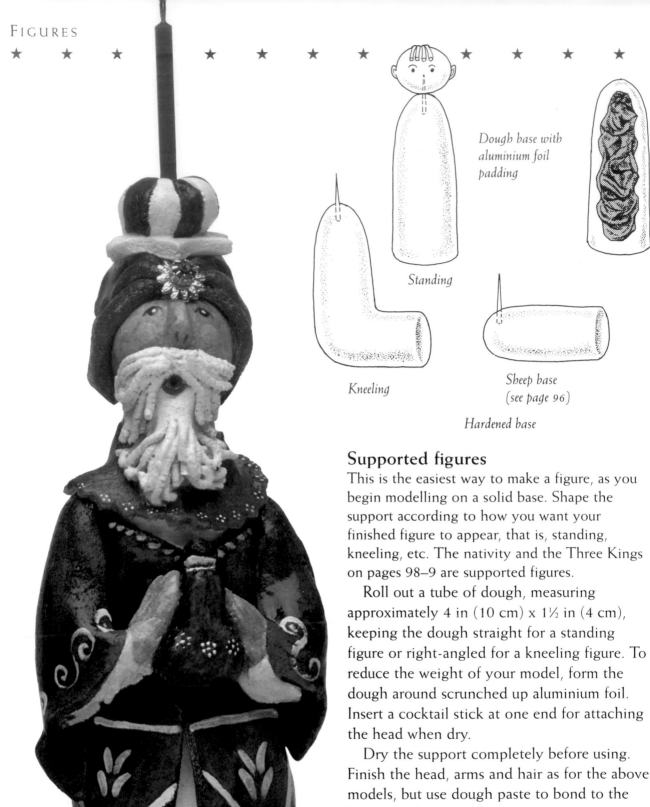

Dough base with aluminium foil padding

Standing

Kneeling

Sheep base (see page 96)

Hardened base

24

Supported figures

This is the easiest way to make a figure, as you begin modelling on a solid base. Shape the support according to how you want your finished figure to appear, that is, standing, kneeling, etc. The nativity and the Three Kings on pages 98–9 are supported figures.

Roll out a tube of dough, measuring approximately 4 in (10 cm) x 1½ in (4 cm), keeping the dough straight for a standing figure or right-angled for a kneeling figure. To reduce the weight of your model, form the dough around scrunched up aluminium foil. Insert a cocktail stick at one end for attaching the head when dry.

Dry the support completely before using. Finish the head, arms and hair as for the above models, but use dough paste to bond to the hardened shape.

You can dress the models with dough or fabric clothes. See the nativity or fairy for further inspiration and technique.

★ ★ ★ ★ ★ ★

Dressing figures

Before making the clothes, consider the
final look of the figure. You may want the
undergarments to show; for example, the
knickerbockers for the doll on page 52.
Always work from the undergarments to the
outer clothing. Lay the greaseproof paper
over the body and mark the relevant details:
armholes, necklines, etc. (see diagram for
method). Cut out patterns from the paper
and then use them to cut clothes from
thinly rolled dough. Moisten each layer of
clothing first before adding it to the
figure. Finely detailed clothing makes the
figure look more authentic, for example,
pockets, collars, belts, buttons, stitching,
etc. For pleats and folds, gather the dough
and press it together, then support it from
beneath to help keep its position.

*Outline clothes on
to tracing paper*

25

CHAPTER FOUR

Finishing Techniques

Impressions made in dough

Make your own pattern mould by cutting a design in linoleum or sculpt a modelling medium such as Fimo or a similar product. For the latter, follow the manufacturer's instructions for the method. You can use shaped butter or cookie moulds, carved or tooled metal, shaped buttons or even the teeth of a comb. Try using textured fabric, such as lace, to add an innovative dimension to your work. Experiment with anything that gives the surface of the dough a unique impression.

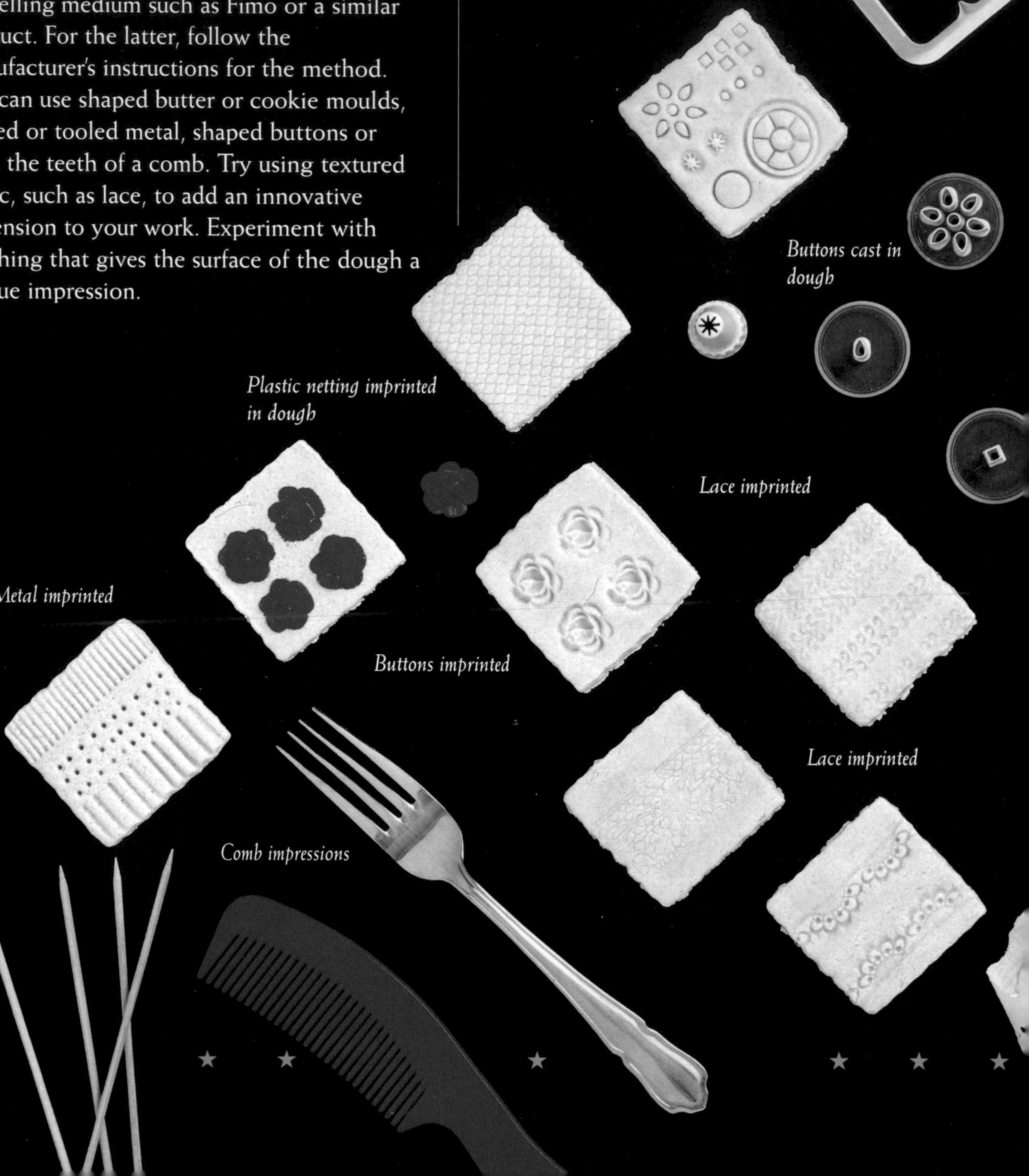

26

Buttons cast in dough

Plastic netting imprinted in dough

Lace imprinted

Metal imprinted

Buttons imprinted

Lace imprinted

Comb impressions

Sieved dough

Nozzles and cotton reels

Brooch imprinted

Garlic press

27

Textures and three-dimensional shapes

As already mentioned, the garlic press can be used for making hair and so on. Experiment with other tools such as sieves, children's play tools and icing equipment to achieve different effects. The photograph illustrates how you can easily achieve interesting surfaces to your work.

High relief

There are many ways to increase the dimension of your work, the simplest being to add flowers, leaves or fruit. You can make attractive garlands using these items. See the examples on pages 83–90 for further inspiration.

Braid imprinted

Lace imprint dusted with gold powder

Leaves, flowers, fruit

Use a leaf-shaped cutter to stamp out a leaf from the dough, or cut one out with a sharp knife and mark the veins with its pointed tip.

Petal shapes

Stages for making a rose

To make flowers, use a flower-shaped icing cutter, or fashion individual petals to form your own flowers.

Model a rose by flattening a small ball of dough between the thumb and index finger and roll it into a coiled tube. Form five or six small pieces into balls, flatten in the palm of your hand and pinch the base of each to a point. Press the top edges between index finger and thumb to frill out the edges. Moisten the rolled tube and gradually add the petals around the tube, overlapping each petal as you go. Trim excess dough on the base with a sharp knife.

Fruit shapes

The easiest shapes to make are apples, oranges, plums, cherries, grapes and berries, as you make them from varying sized balls of dough simply by rolling in the palm of your hand. Insert cloves for stems or buds of fruit. Fuse wire

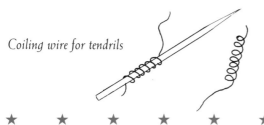

Coiling wire for tendrils

Primrose shape

coiled around thin dowelling makes ideal grape tendrils (see diagram).

Bend a piece of wire in half to make stems for cherries. Indent the surface of oranges or tangerines with a star-shaped nozzle or cheese grater to reproduce the pitted effect. To make bananas, curve a dough tube to a half moon shape, pinching together at one end to form the shape of the stem.

28

Weaving dough strips for baskets

Woven textures

For a basket weave effect cut a thinly rolled sheet of dough into strips. Lay strips vertically and horizontally, weaving one strip over the other on top of the hardened base as illustrated. Trim away excess dough from the edges curving into a basket shape.

Fish scales

Cut pointed U-shapes from thinly rolled dough to make fish scales. Lay one U-shape next to another in a row, on the next row lay one in the middle of the two above, and so on.

Fish scales

Spines/feathers

Spines, for example, on a hedgehog's back, or a bird's feathers can be made by cutting a V-shape in the dough with small pointed scissors.

Snip dough with scissors for spines or feathers

Baking and drying the dough

Air-drying

This is the cheapest method. It is ideally suited for drying thin models or plaques. Leave the shapes on a tray to dry in the air. You can dry your work in the garden, first putting it in the shade and then in the sun as it hardens. Watch out for predators, such as squirrels, which may nibble at your samples! Bring your work in at night, as mist will soften it. You will also need to allow several days before the dough is completely dry: the colour lightens as it dries. Air-drying can make the base retract, so remember to turn the pieces regularly. Thicker shapes may be air-dried, but the process will take several weeks. Bear this in mind if you want your pieces for a specific occasion. Your work can be dried on a wire grill, over a radiator or in an airing cupboard. Thick models that are first air-dried must be finished off in a cool oven, approximately 110°C/225°F, Gas Mark ½ to 140°C/275°F, Gas Mark 1.

Oven drying

Oven temperatures and times vary according to how your oven is heated.

Slow cool drying

This method takes between 8–12 hours at a temperature of 50°C/100°F, Gas Mark minimum to 75°C/150°F, Gas Mark ¼, and is well suited to electric ovens. For fan-assisted ovens use the lower temperature. Slow cooking is ideal for thin or small items. Turn the shapes over half way through the drying process. Delicate shapes may need extra support in the oven with scrunched aluminium foil.

In the case of gas ovens it may be necessary to prop the oven door open, as the heat is much fiercer. The drying time in gas ovens is usually half that of electric ovens. Keep an eye on your work to prevent it from browning too much.

Quicker drying

It is possible to increase the oven temperature after the first couple of hours, but do not exceed 150°C/300°F, Gas Mark 2. This is suitable for small, thin pieces only.

The oven drying time and temperature really depends on your own particular oven model. Sometimes the insulation has worn in older ovens allowing heat to escape, so experiment with different thicknesses of dough to gauge the best results from your oven. As a rule, allow half an hour per ¼ in (6 mm) thickness of dough. To economise on your electricity or gas bill, make sure your oven is full of exciting ideas: you can reproduce a tiered system for your drying by using wire racks.

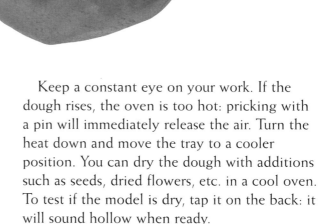

Keep a constant eye on your work. If the dough rises, the oven is too hot: pricking with a pin will immediately release the air. Turn the heat down and move the tray to a cooler position. You can dry the dough with additions such as seeds, dried flowers, etc. in a cool oven. To test if the model is dry, tap it on the back: it will sound hollow when ready.

Remember to use oven gloves as the dough is very hot when dry. So once you are sure the dough is dry, remove it from the oven and cool on a wire rack. To prevent edges curling, weight them down with a flat, heavy object.

Painting dough

You can paint the dough before or after drying. Use watercolour paints or marker pens, hobby paints such as enamels, or water soluble poster paints. Paints with a water base are best for children to use as they are non-toxic and do not require a spirit solvent to clean the brushes. Watercolours have a delightful translucent quality if applied to the dough. For a solid colour, coat the model with a base coat of primer. Allow the painted model to dry thoroughly before you varnish it. Use wide brushes for large areas and fine ones for detailing. Bend the end of the brush to paint the edges of rounded surfaces: to do this, leave a brush standing in water until the ends curve over.

32

Drying coloured dough

A slow drying process is the best method to keep the colours true, so do not have the oven hotter than 100°C/200°F, Gas Mark ¼–½ at the final drying stage.

Baked bread effect

Browning dough gives it an attractive rustic look, imitating the delicious appearance of home-baked bread. First turn the oven up to 200°C/400°F, Gas Mark 6. Using a brush, paint the piece to be browned with a salt-water solution. Dry the model in the oven for 10 minutes, and when dry coat with a wash of egg and milk. Experiment with the cooking times to vary the shading of the dough.

Varnishing

It is necessary to varnish salt dough once the model is completed, thereby helping to preserve and protect it and ensuring your work will last for several years. A varnished surface can easily be kept clean with a damp cloth. There are different varnishes on the market to suit the end use. Check with your hobby or craft shop that the varnish you buy is compatible with the paint used. Clear polyurethane varnishes such as those used for boats and floors are ideal for natural looking models and the back of your work. Varnish comes in matt or gloss, and there is a brown tint even to polyurethane clear varnish. For a transparent effect use watercolour varnish: this is excellent used over white paint. Give your models at least two coats of varnish on both sides to ensure they are properly covered. Let the varnish work its way through the textured surfaces such as the hair.

Be sure to air your room when you are using varnishes and spirits, as they give off strong vapours that could be harmful if inhaled for long periods. Keep varnishes away from a naked flame and children.

33

Backing models

To neaten the backs of your models, cut a piece of felt to size and glue on. You can stick felt discs to the base of your model to protect your table tops from getting scratched.

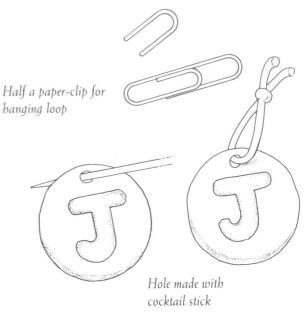

Half a paper-clip for hanging loop

Hole made with cocktail stick

Hanging

There are several methods to use depending on the weight of the model. Break a wire paper-clip in half and embed it in the dough at the top or back. This method suits most models. For heavier plaques use a 4 in (10 cm) piece of string folded in half as a hanging loop secured to the back with pieces of dough. You can stick linen picture hooks on the back to hang lightweight models. Check the recommended weight load indicated on the pack. To make a hole in the dough for a hanging thread use the blunt end of a cocktail stick. A wire paper-clip is adequate for hanging the ice-skater, modelled on the figure technique in Chapter 3.

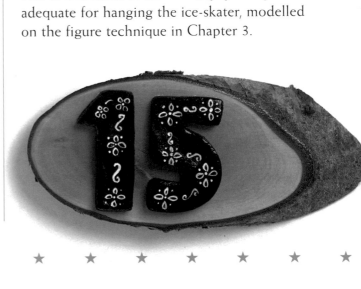

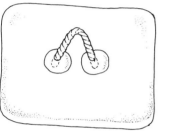

Half paper-clip hook

*Adhesive linen
picture hook*

*String and dough
hook*

Storage

Moisture is the main cause of your model becoming dull or softening. It is best to display models in an even temperature. Do not exhibit them near direct heat, as this may cause them to warp or crack. Doughcrafted models are not suitable for permanent use out of doors, but will be all right in a porchway.

Wipe your models with a duster from time to time to keep the colours bright or use a hair drier to remove dust from delicate detailing.

Problem solving

Your models may crack in the oven when drying or with general wear and tear. To reduce damage occuring in the oven, prick air bubbles with a pin to release air during cooking, and reduce oven temperature (see page 81).

Do not discard cracked models, as it is easy to repair them. A paste made from dough and water is perfect for most minor repairs: fill the crack with the paste and allow it to air-dry. Touch up obvious joins with paint to match the colour of the finished article, then varnish the join. Give the whole model a coat of varnish to freshen it up.

★ ★ ★ ★ ★ ★ ★ ★ ★ ★ ★ ★ ★ ★ ★ ★

Gift Ideas for Adults

Couple in bed plaque
Measures 8 in (20 cm) x 7 in (17 cm)

This makes an amusing gift for a couple. Style
and colour the hair to match that of the
recipient, or add extra features, such as glasses if
worn. Colour the quilt and sheets to correspond
with the couple's own bedroom decor.

The bed
Roll out half the quantity of the basic recipe to
the above measurements, and ¼ in (6 mm) thick.
Place the rolled dough on a tray lined with
baking parchment and round off the bottom
edge by cutting away the excess dough with a
knife. Make two oblongs of dough, each 2½ in
(6 cm) x 1½ in (4 cm) x 1 in (2.5 cm) thick for

★ ★ ★ ★

the pillows. Roll out two strips of dough about 10 in (25 cm) x ¾ in (2 cm) x ⅛ in (2.5 mm) thick for pillow frills. Scallop one long edge of each strip using a scallop-shaped cake cutter. Moisten the edges of each pillow piece with water. Gather the frills as you attach them around the outer edges on each pillow. Prick three dots in each scallop with the point of a cocktail stick to achieve a broderie anglaise pattern. Position the lace pillows on the base sheet of the bed.

The couple
Model two balls of dough, each 1¼ in (3 cm) in diameter, for the heads. Make two bodies 3 in (8 cm) x 1½ in (4 cm); fix two small dough balls for breasts on to the female with water. Join the heads to the bodies, and make hair for each figure, using a garlic press. Moisten the figures with water and lay the heads of each half figure in the middle of the pillows. Outline the body shape on tracing paper for each figure, and use the tracing at a later stage for pyjamas and nightdress. Make arms and hands as for the figures on page 19 and join at the shoulder of each figure.

Cut out the pyjama and nightdress shapes from rolled dough, following the features illustration on page 22. Dress the figures, making sure that the lower edge of the clothes finish just below the edge of the sheet.

Roll out a piece of dough 8 in (20 cm) square for the quilt and scallop top edge. Fold the scalloped edge of the sheet back 1½ in (4 cm), moisten the under-side and lay it over the figures. Pleat the dough sheet to resemble the folds in a quilt. Shape two small balls of equal size into a pair of feet, fashion toes from ten tiny balls of dough and secure five toes to each foot with water. Form a piece of dough 1½ in (4 cm) square x ¼ in (6 mm) thick for the open book, fold in half and position as in the illustration. Arrange the hands as illustrated. Additional detailing, such as lace on the nightdress, and spectacles, are added when the model has been hardened. Make the spectacles from florist's wire (see diagram on page 22).

Name plaques
Roll a flat sheet of dough measuring 4½ in (12 cm) long x 2¼ in (6 cm) wide x ¼ in (6 mm) thick; curve the corners with a sharp knife. Make a head and model it, using the features ideas on pages 22–3, to represent the face of the person who is to receive the plaque. Fix the head on to the right-hand side of the plaque with water. Make a hanging attachment from a paper-clip, or pierce a hole through the top at the centre with a cocktail stick (see hanging instructions on page 34). Write the person's name on the plaque in paint, felt pen or adhesive lettering.

37

38

Mannequin and weight lifter
Height 8 in (20 cm)

Both figures are modelled as for the figure on page 19. Paint the underwear or swimsuit as illustrated. Glue the lace trim and bow to the completed female figure. Glue a bamboo skewer to the hands of the male figure and a wooden bead at each end for the weights.

Jewellery ideas

Primrose necklace and earrings

Cut two large and two small flowers using primrose-shaped icing cutters. For the necklace, glue the petals of the large flowers over each other with water; pierce a hole in the centre for the stamen with a cocktail stick. Make a hanging loop from a tiny tube of dough and fix the loop to the top of the under-side of the flower with water. Make a hole with a bamboo skewer in the centre of each small petal. When hard, paint each petal primrose yellow and glue a stamen in the centre of each one. Finish by varnishing, and glue an earring stud to the back of each small flower. Thread green ribbon through the loop on the pendant and knot the ends of the ribbon to make a necklace.

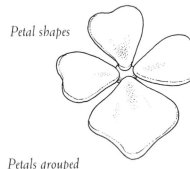

Petal shapes

Petals grouped together with stamen inserted in centre

Pansy brooch

Pansy brooch

Make three petals approximately 1 in (2.5 cm) long from small balls of dough, and one petal 1½ in (4 cm) long. Overlap the three smaller petals in a fan shape and moisten with water to secure. Lay the edge of these over the large petal shape and pinch all the petals together at the base in the centre. Pierce a hole through the middle of the flower with a cocktail stick for the stamen. Paint the flower as illustrated or use a real flower to copy the colourings. Glue the stamen into the hole so that it protrudes by ¼ in (6 mm). Attach a brooch clip on the reverse with strong glue.

Acorn brooch

Make two acorns and two oak leaves following the garland method on page 86. Tie a 10 in (25 cm) × ¼ in (6 mm) length of gold cord into a bow; glue the top of the acorn cups to each of the bow ends. Glue the middle of the bow to the stems of the leaves. Attach a brooch clasp to the back of the cord bow.

40

Key holders

You can make simple key holders by using shaped cookie cutters to cut the base from dough ½ in (12 mm) thick. Indent the dough with the end of a screw hook; the number of key hooks required will be determined by the size and shape of the base. Paint the front of the holder with floral or geometric patterns. When dry, screw in the hooks and glue a fabric-hanging loop on to the back.

Attach a purchased key-ring to a hardened heart-shaped piece of dough that has a hole made in it for the purpose.

★ ★ ★ ★ ★ ★ ★ ★ ★ ★ ★

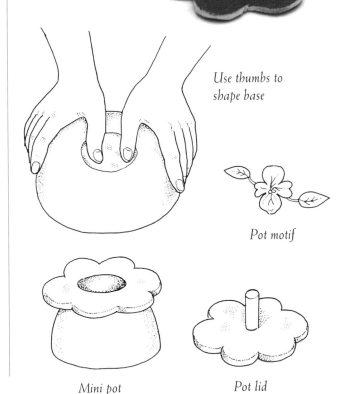

41

Mini pot

Height 2 in (5 cm)

Small pots make useful gifts for
holding bits and bobs in the office
or kitchen.

   Indent a large ball of stiff dough with your
thumbs and thin the outer ring at the top by
squeezing it between the thumb and fingers.
Press thumbs down in the middle of the ball,
and push the dough out at the base, circling the
dough as you work, to form the hollow base.
Cut a petal shape with a cookie cutter; remove
the centre with an icing nozzle and stick it on
to the top of the base. Smooth the inner rim
with moistened fingers. Make a pot lid from a
piece of dough cut with a petal-shaped cutter
and attach a stalk made from a tiny tube of
dough for lifting the lid off the pot. Paint the
hardened pot and lid with the violet design as
illustrated.

*Use thumbs to
shape base*

Pot motif

Mini pot

Pot lid

Love spoons

Length 8 in (20 cm)

Roll a piece of dough to an oblong ¼ in (6 mm) thick and longer than the spoon and mould an oval piece of dough for the spoon bowl. Brush the front of the spoon with oil, cut baking parchment to fit the handle and stick down. Make an oval shape from parchment to fit the spoon bowl and snip around the edges so it lies flat. Lay the oblong of dough over the spoon, press the oval piece of dough in the spoon bowl, and trim overlapping pieces with a sharp knife. Decorate as illustrated, with twists and cut heart shapes. For a realistic wood effect use brown-coloured dough, or paint brown.

42

Fir tree jewellery

Length of necklace 12 in (30 cm)
Length of earrings 2 in (5 cm)

Use a cutter to make the shapes. The beads are tiny balls of dough threaded on string.

Hair combs

Height 2½ in (7 cm)

Decorate hair combs with rose-buds, or for festive cheer use holly and berries. Attach hardened trims with a strong glue.

Santa 'Daddy' resting
Height 8 in (20 cm)

First of all, make the sofa and harden it before working on the Santa figure.

Construct a box-shaped support frame from balsa wood or strong cardboard. The frame needs to measure 8 in (20 cm) long × 4 in (10 cm) wide × 5 in (12 cm) high.

Roll two tubes of dough 1¼ in (3 cm) in diameter × 4 in (10 cm) long for the arm rests. Make two small flattened discs for the ends of the arms and fix in position with water. Shape the back of the chair from dough as in the illustration and join the arms to it. Dry this section in the oven before attaching it to the sofa base.

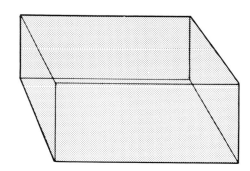

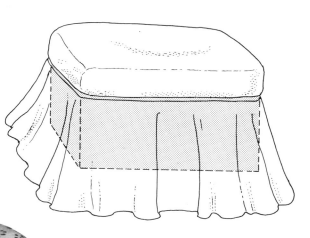

Dough moulded over card support

Cut a circular piece of dough 12 in (30 cm) in diameter and about ½ in (12 mm) thick for the sofa frill. Scallop the edge of the circular skirt with a shaped cutter and cover the frame with it, pinching the dough into gathers. Make an oblong cushion to fit on the top of the frame to a depth of ¾ in (2 cm). Position the top sofa section on to the hardened base and secure with dough.

Press the two pieces firmly together. Model a small cushion from a cube of dough and place it in one corner of the sofa, shaping it into position. Harden the sofa in the oven and support the back of the sofa as in the diagram with a bamboo skewer.

Assemble the figure using the method on page 19. Give Santa a knitted hat, made from a length of tubular knitting gathered at one end with a pom-pom sewn on top, some mince pies on a plate and a doll's house sized bottle of whisky.

Model the cat in the arm chair, using the same method as the sofa.

Santa's sleigh
Length 12 in (30 cm)

Use the template on pages 118–19 to cut out two sides for the sleigh from dough rolled to a thickness of ½ in (12 mm). Make a base and two end sections from the given measurements. Assemble the sides, base and ends with glue, using a glue gun. Decorate the hardened sleigh by gluing on a braid trim, and fill it with gold-wrapped chocolate coins. (For illustration see pages 44–5.)

Prop back of chair with cocktail stick during drying process

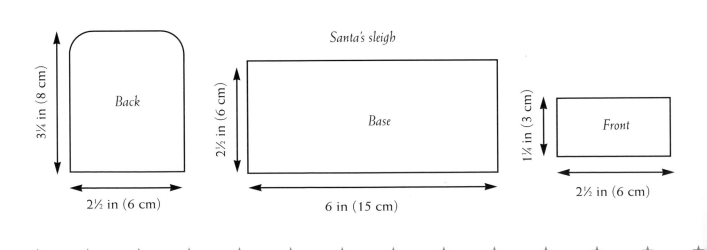

Santa's sleigh

3¼ in (8 cm)

Back

2½ in (6 cm)

2½ in (6 cm)

Base

6 in (15 cm)

1¼ in (3 cm)

Front

2½ in (6 cm)

★ ★ ★ ★ ★ ★ ★ ★ ★ ★ ★ ★ ★ ★ ★

Poinsettia in basket
Measures 12 in (30 cm) x 8 in (20 cm)

Roll out half the quantity of dough into a
flat sheet ¼ in (6 mm) thick. Divide the
dough into strips about ¾ in (2 cm) wide.
Line a cookie sheet with baking parchment,
lay strips of dough vertically on the sheet,
take another strip of dough and weave it over
and under the vertical strips. The size of the
basket will decide the number of strips you
require. Shape the weaving into a three-quarter
circle by cutting away the excess dough with a
sharp knife.

Roll some dough into two ¾ in (2 cm)
thick tubes that are long enough to form the
handle of the basket; gauge the length from
the width of the basket. Twist the tubes
together and secure at each side of the
basket with water. Fix a strip of dough
1½ in (4 cm) deep along the top
edge of the basket to act as a
base for the artificial
poinsettia flowers.
When hard, glue on the
artificial flowers. Paint
the basket with gold-
coloured enamel.
Finish off by tying a
gold bow around the
handle, turning it into
a special gift.

47

★ ★ ★ ★ ★ ★ ★ ★ ★ ★ ★ ★ ★ ★ ★ ★ ★

The farmer and his wife
Height 9 in (23 cm)

Roll two balls of dough for the heads and lay these on a cookie sheet lined with parchment. Make two body shapes (see page 18 for method). Gather the dough to make the wife's underskirt and give her apron a scalloped edge; these pieces are positioned before the arms and sleeves. Model her shoes from two equal-sized balls of dough pinched at the end to form clogs.

Divide some hair strands at the centre and drape around the head, and fashion a small ball of dough into a bun.

The farmer has a smock over his breeches, and you will need to make the pants first. Use the ideas on pages 22–3 as a guide. The farmer's crook is a forked piece of twig embedded in the palm of his hand. To hang the figures, use two halves of a paper-clip and insert one in the top of the head of each figure.

★ ★ ★ ★ ★ ★ ★ ★ ★ ★ ★ ★ ★ ★ ★ ★ ★

★ ★ ★ ★ ★ ★ ★ ★ ★ ★ ★ ★ ★ ★ ★ ★

Grandpa and Grandma
Measures 10 in (25 cm) square

Roll half the basic recipe to a flat sheet
¼ in (6 mm) thick, and from it cut the outline of
the house and the shutters with a craft knife.
Make the roof tiles from strips of dough cut
with a scalloped edge cutter. Lay the strips over
each other, making sure that the scallop on the
lower row meets the middle of the one above.
Roll a long strip and two narrow strips of
dough for the window-box. Model the
top halves of a male and a female figure
(see page 36). Position the couple in the
open window behind the sill.

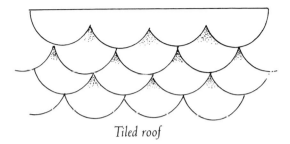

Tiled roof

Glue net curtains behind the couple as shown
in the illustration. Fashion knitting in
Grandma's hands from two cocktail
sticks and make Grandpa's spectacles
using the method for the couple in
bed plaque (see page 36).

49

★ ★ ★ ★ ★

Cat on a window box plaque
Height 9 in (23 cm)

Begin with the window frame. Strengthen the ends of the cross-section with cocktail sticks inserted in the dough to support it. Model the cat from two balls of dough and fix it on the windowsill with water. Make a window-box from flat strips of dough, supported from beneath with scraps of dough so that the box is not flush against the sill. Insert a paper-clip loop at the top of the frame. Glue some dry flowers into the

window-box once the plaque has been varnished and allow to dry.

Cut two strips of gingham fabric the width of the window and 1 in (2.5 cm) longer for the curtains. Run a gathering thread along the top of each strip and draw both up to half their width. Slightly overlap the two pieces in the middle, glue the back of the frame down at the cross-section and lay on top of the curtains. Trim away excess fabric from the top and bottom before securing the lower edge of fabric to the back of the frame with a layer of glue.

Strengthen frame

50

51

Cross-section of
butcher's hat

Butcher's hat

The butcher, the baker, the candlestick maker
Height 9 in (23 cm)

Make the three figures using the method described on page 18. Fashion the clothes before the arms. Use the features ideas on pages 22–3 to add details to the characters. You can purchase miniature candlesticks from doll's house suppliers or by mail order.

Make the butcher's boater from plaited straw glued on to a circle of card that has the middle removed. Cover the top of a 1½ in (4 cm)

diameter plastic lid with plaited straw to make the crown and glue another piece around the side. Glue the crown over the brim, and fix some ribbon around the side of the boater. Cut the completed hat in a half cross-section and glue it to the head (see illustration).

★ ★ ★ ★ ★ ★ ★ ★ ★ ★ ★ ★ ★ ★ ★ ★

CHAPTER SIX

Gift Ideas for Childre

Victorian Miss

Height 12 in (30 cm)

Model the body according to the instructions for the flat figure on page 18, using bamboo skewers for extra support. Shape the feet to resemble pointed ballet shoes and gather an oblong piece of dough over them for the knickerbockers. Pleat a large oblong of dough over the knickerbockers for the skirt and a smaller oblong on top for the apron. Small dough gathers form the frilled sleeves. Model the hat as shown in the diagram. Make a hole in the middle of the hands to insert some dry or artificial flowers after the model has been painted. When the model has hardened, paint it, and for extra embellishment glue lace on to the hat and apron, add ribbon bows to the hair and ribbon roses to the shoes. Glue flowers into the hands.

Crescent shape forms hat brim

Model the basic hat shape as shown here

★ ★ ★ ★ ★ ★ ★ ★ ★ ★ ★ ★

Toy Soldier

Height 12 in (30 cm)

You can make a cheerful toy soldier using the flat figure method of modelling on page 18. It is advisable to support the limbs and head with pieces of bamboo skewer cut to size, inserting them at the end of the limbs and head piece and joining them to the appropriate part of the body. A paper-clip loop is sufficient to hang a small figure. As our soldier is fairly heavy, he has a string loop attached to the back of the figure (for the method see page 34). Paint the hardened figure in bright colours following the photograph, or use your little boy's favourite soldier as a guide. Additional trims make the soldier more realistic, such as medals and epaulettes. The epaulettes are made from lampshade fringing glued on to the figure after varnishing. Cut two lengths of braid, each about 4 in (10 cm) long and glue one piece around each shoulder. Glue a small piece of braid at the top of the epaulette, filling in the gap.

53

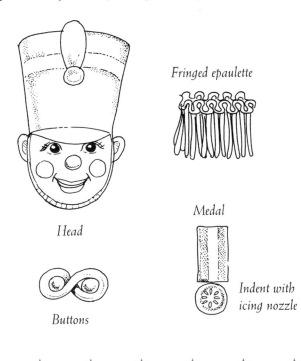

Head

Fringed epaulette

Buttons

Medal

Indent with icing nozzle

"T" Shape for clown's jumpsuit

Gather cuffs

Gather cuffs

54

Jolly clown
Height 12 in (30 cm)

Make the body shape using the figure method on page 18. As the clown wears a jumbo-sized play-suit, the body needs to have extra dough padding. Roll a sheet of dough out to ¼ in (6 mm) thick, sufficiently long and wide to reach both hands and feet; from it cut out a T-shaped piece of dough as shown in the line illustration. Slice the dough up the middle for the division of each leg piece. Lay the shaped dough over the padded body and squeeze the dough into pleats at the wrists and ankles. Cut out shoes with extra long fronts to them.

The cuff and ankle ruffles are made from dough cut with a star-shaped cutter; remove the middle of the star with a knife to enable it to be wrapped around the arms and legs.

Clown pendant

Length 2 in (5 cm)

Roll and flatten a ball of dough for
the clown's head and dress with
hair. Insert a hanging loop made
from a paper-clip into the top
and thread a ribbon through it.

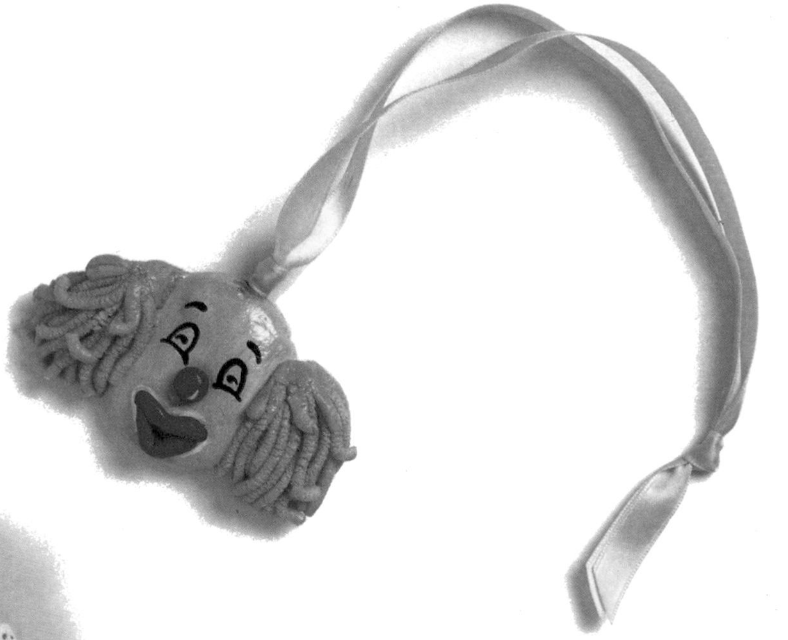

Sunday best

Height 10 in (25 cm)

Model the girl using the flat figure method
on page 18. Make the knickerbockers before
the coat. The hat is fashioned from a
crescent-shaped piece of dough: scallop the
outer edge with a cutter (see the diagram).
Use a cocktail stick to print holes
resembling broderie anglaise on the hat
and knickerbockers. Insert a paper-clip
into the top of the head for hanging.

Sleeping rabbit

Rabbit asleep in a moon hammock

Height 10 in (25 cm)

Roll dough into a flat sheet ¼ in (6 mm) thick. Cut a crescent-shaped piece of dough 12 in (30 cm) long, and 3½ in (9 cm) at the widest point. Form a piece of dough into a 1½ in (4 cm) ball for the head and secure it to the inner edge of the crescent shape with water. Shape a 4 in (10 cm) tube of dough for the body. Snip one end where the legs divide and mould dough into feet at the end of each leg. Secure the top of the body below the head and arch the back to fit the inner curve of the moon. Add arms and features at this stage. Cut the holly and the stocking out of scraps of dough and attach to the plaque.

Make a hole at the top of the plaque for a ribbon hanging loop with a blunt end of a bamboo skewer.

This would make a lovely gift for a new-born baby: paint the clothes blue for a boy or pink for a girl. Hang the plaque on the outside of the nursery door if you want to show that the baby is sleeping.

★ ★ ★ ★ ★ ★ ★ ★ ★ ★ ★ ★ ★ ★ ★

Babushka doll
Height 9 in (23 cm)

Use the template from the pattern section on
page 120 to cut the outline for the doll from a
½ in (12 mm) thick sheet of dough. Remove the
face section as illustrated, roll a ball of dough to
fit the cut out section and slightly flatten it
into a dome shape. Roll a piece of dough
6 in (15 cm) x 3 in (8 cm) for the body;
fashion two small balls into breast shapes
and secure into position
with water.

Place the stomach piece in the
centre of a lined cookie sheet and
position the face 1½ in (4 cm)
above it. Moisten the under-side
of the flat outlined piece of dough
and lay dampened side over the
other two pieces. Using your
thumbs, press the cut out shape
around the face and stomach.
Using a cookie cutter, cut out a
scalloped border for the apron and
place over the raised stomach in a U-
shape to form the apron. Using the
point of a kitchen knife, outline the top
half of the apron and the hair parting.
Add remaining details before drying. Insert
half a paper-clip into the top for the loop.

For an entertaining wall hanging, make a
series of dolls that diminish in size, representing
the doll-within-a-doll idea. Use the same
template as for the Babushka doll but decorate
it to make a tubby Santa.

57

Babushka doll

Santa

★ ★ ★ ★ ★ ★

Piggy-bank

Height 5 in (12.5 cm)

You will need two bowl-shaped pieces of dough to form the body of the pig: rice-bowls are ideal for this purpose. Use a 1½ in (4 cm) diameter plastic lid as the stopper for the money in the pig: cardboard poster tubes have lids suitable for this purpose.

Brush the bowl with cooking oil and place a 12 in (30 cm) long x 1 in (2.5 cm) wide length of baking parchment over the bowl for a lifting tab. Roll half the basic recipe into a flat sheet ½ in (12 mm) thick. Cut a 10 in (25 cm) diameter circle from the dough, lay the circle of dough over the upturned bowl and mould it around the bowl, smoothing out any bumps. Trim overlapping dough from the base of the bowl to make a neat edge.

Dry the shape in the oven. Before it hardens, cut a slit ¾ in (2 cm) long for inserting coins on one side of the bowl and a semicircle on the opposite side to fit the plastic lid.

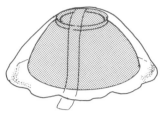

Upturned rice bowl

1/2 section cut for coins and lid

Joined up pig

Remove the shape from the mould by gently pulling the parchment tabs and easing it off with a knife.

Make a second half to match. Check that the openings line up and join the two hardened halves with dough paste. Support the oval shape with scrunched up aluminium foil and dry it in the oven. When hardened and cooled, smooth any roughness around the join with fine sandpaper.

Roll a ball of dough measuring 3½ in (9 cm) for the head. Fashion ears from two small balls of dough about 1½ in (4 cm) diameter. Shape the nose and mouth as shown in the photograph and attach the head to the body with dough paste. Press two peppercorns in the dough head for eyes. Shape two balls of dough into trotter shapes and position them at the front of the pig. Twist a 4 in (10 cm) length of pipe cleaner into a spiral for the pig's tail. Glue the tail on to the pig after varnishing.

★ ★ ★ ★ ★ ★

Cat napping
Length 8 in (20 cm)

You can make the cat from one piece of dough. Model in the same manner as the figure shown on page 20. The head, legs and arms are all moulded from the body portion of dough. Shape the ends of the limbs into paws. Make a tail from a tube of dough; attach to the body with water. Mould two small balls into pointed ear shapes and attach to each side of the head. Whiskers are made from black-painted fuse wire. Bend arms and legs so that the cat reclines in a backward position.

Teddy bear
Height 4 in (10 cm)

This cute little bear is made from a small dough ball for the head and a larger ball to form the body. Tubes of dough are used for the arms and legs. Press a small disc of dough to the lower part of the face for the snout and slit it down the middle with a knife. Roll a tiny ball of dough for the nose and attach at the top of the snout. Indent each ear with the blunt end of a bamboo skewer and mark the eyes with the pointed end.

Hedgehog and mouse

Length 4 in (10 cm)

Roll dough into a 4 in (10 cm) ball. Pinch the ball at one end between thumb and index finger to form the tapered nose of a mouse or hedgehog. Make a tiny nose, and a pair of ears for the mouse from two small petal-shaped pieces of dough. Press two peppercorns into the dough for eyes. Snip across the back of the hedgehog with scissors to make the spines. To complete the mouse, glue a string tail on to the hardened body. Paint the mouse. Glaze and brown the hedgehog to achieve a rustic look.

Name plaque

Measures 4 in (10 cm) x 2½ in (6.5 cm)

Roll out a ¼ in (6 mm) thick sheet of dough to the above measurements. Model the head on the features of the child receiving the gift, matching hair, freckles, etc. Position the head on the right-hand side of the plaque and secure with water. After varnishing, paint or use adhesive lettering to write the name of the child on the plaque. Glue linen hanging loops on the reverse of the plaque to hang on a door.

★ ★ ★ ★ ★ ★ ★ ★ ★ ★ ★ ★ ★ ★ ★ ★ ★

Owl

Height 10 in (25 cm)

Line a large cookie tray with baking parchment. Flatten an oval of dough measuring 5 in (12.5 cm) wide x 4 in (10 cm) deep x ½ in (12 mm) at the edges to ¾ in (2 cm) in the middle for the face. Roll an elongated oval shape for the body measuring 6 in (15 cm) deep x 5 in (12.5 cm) wide x ½ in (12 mm) thick and join to the head with a cocktail stick. Form two wings from dough as shown in the photograph and secure a wing to each side of the body with water. Snip the bottom edge of the body to form tail feathers. The feather surrounds for the eyes are dried wild fungi pushed into the dough to make an impression, then glued on when hard. Fashion a beak shape to go in the centre of the fungi. Roll two small balls for feet and snip each ball with scissors three times to make the owl's claws; dry the feet separately and glue on the stem of the branch after the varnishing process. Before drying, imprint the stem about 1 in (2.5 cm) up from the tip of the tail feathers to mark the spot for the owl to perch.

Before drying the model, snip the dough to create the feathers on the wings, body and head sections. Lift the cut section up as you snip the dough. Make some long feathers for the eyebrows.

Be careful not to damage the feathers when painting and varnishing the owl.

★ ★ ★ ★ ★ ★ ★ ★ ★ ★ ★ ★ ★ ★

Train plaque

Measures 6 in (15 cm) x 12 in (30 cm)

Roll dough to a flat sheet ¼ in (6 mm) thick.
Trace the train template (see pages 122–3) on
to stiff card and cut out. Lay the card outline on
the dough and using a sharp craft knife cut away
the protruding dough. Take care that you do not
stretch the dough when cutting out the shape.
Lift the train shape on to a flat cookie sheet
with a fish slice. From the remaining scraps of
dough make wheel guards and form small balls
of dough for the wheel centres. Cut a flat piece
of dough into a funnel for the chimney.

You can turn this into an extra special
personalized gift for a little boy by adding
dough letters along the side of the train to
form the child's name. Use alphabet cutters for
the letters, or stencil them on – perhaps in a
variety of colours – after you have painted the
train and allowed the paint to dry.

The edges of the train must be weighted
down during the drying process to prevent
them from curling. Use adhesive linen
hooks for hanging your plaque, or make
holes on both sides of the train at the top
edge for a hanging cord before drying the
train in the oven.

62

Letters of the alphabet

Height 4 in (10 cm)

Letters are made from tubes of dough about
¾ in (2 cm) diameter. Join the cross-sections of
the letters with water. Decorate the letters with
toy shapes, dough children, or flowers made
using icing cutters. Initials make a perfect gift
for a child's bedroom door. To hang the letter
insert half a paper-clip into the top. You
can make a child's name from dough
letters. Glue the letters on to a
length of varnished pine-wood
for a special present.

National costumes
Average height 6 in (15 cm)

Model figures using the flat figure method in Chapter 3. To add more detail, use the features ideas on pages 22–3 as your guide. All models need paper-clip hanging loops, or glue figures on to a hessian display board to make an attractive wall hanging. The additional detailing for each figure enhances their realism.

Japanese girl

Viking

Eskimo

64

Scot's lass

Scottish lass

The beret can be decorated with a real pom-pom, or make one out of dough. The kilt is fashioned from an oblong piece of dough slit several times at the base to make pleats; paint a tartan design on it once the model has hardened.

Squaw

Plait thin strands of dough for the braids. Glue a feather at the back of the head. Make a bow from a thin, flexible piece of twig and strong thread. For the necklace, thread a few tiny multicoloured beads on to cotton.

Viking

Cut a sword shape from balsa wood, paint it silver and glue it to the hand. Make the designs on the helmet and shield by pressing a star-shaped nozzle into the dough.

Japanese girl

The front of the kimono is modelled from two pieces of dough, one long piece overlapping a shorter piece. Make each sleeve from a triangular sheet of dough folded in half and wrapped around the arm. Glue a ribbon rose and pointed ends of a cocktail stick into the hair.

Eskimo

Press the dough through a fine sieve to reproduce the fur trim on the anorak. Pinch the ends of the dough to make pointed winter boots. Make a fish from a small piece of dough. Use a thin twig as a fishing rod and tie the fish on to it with a piece of strong thread.

Squaw

65

Dutch girl

Model a triangular piece of dough
on the head for the hat, turning
up the brim at the sides. Glue
a milk pail into one hand
(this can be purchased
from doll's house suppliers).

Dutch girl

66

African warrior

Knot raffia over an elastic band for the grass
skirt. To do this, fold a 4¾ in (12 cm) length
of raffia in half. Loop the raffia over and
through the elastic band to form a knot. Repeat
around the elastic band until it is covered. Trim
the ends of the raffia to just above the knees of
the figure. The spear handle is made from a
bamboo skewer.

African warrior

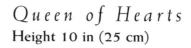

Queen of Hearts
Height 10 in (25 cm)

This plaque shows how illustrations such as those from the delightful book Alice Through the Looking Glass generate excellent ideas for a child's bedroom or nursery. If you do not have this story-book try the local library: it is sure to house a wealth of ideas.

Enlarge the book illustration, using a photocopying machine or graph paper, to the size of model you require and outline the details on tracing paper. Roll a flat sheet of dough ¼ in (6 mm) thick and large enough to fit the tracing. Prick the traced outline on to the dough with a needle and cut the excess dough away with a craft knife. Additional layers of dough are added to give further depth to the skirt, crown, etc. Mark the lines on the face with the point of a bamboo skewer.

67

Mad Hatter
Height 6 in (15 cm)

Make the plaque using the method described for the Queen of Hearts. You need only model the hare's head and shoulders to turn the silhouette into a perfect picture for your frame. Line the backing card of your frame with colour-coordinated paper, and glue the shape in the middle of it. To finish off, the model could be set in a bought picture frame without glass.

CHAPTER SEVEN

Gift Ideas for the Home

Clock face

Measures 11 in (28 cm) square

This is easier to make than it looks! Paint the illustrated motifs on the clock face or make your own design using adhesive transfers; make the numbers the same way. Purchase the clock movement and hands from a craft shop or mail order supplier. You can make a kitchen clock as a special gift for a friend. A teapot silhouette, strawberry outline or sliced vegetable shape such as a green pepper make interesting and amusing dough clocks.

Roll dough combined with wallpaper glue to a flat sheet ¼ in (6 mm) thick. Cut it out to the above measurements, shaping the top into a dome as illustrated. Make a hole ½ in (12 mm) diameter in the centre for fitting the clock movement at the back. Harden the sheet in the oven and weight down its edges during drying to prevent them from curling.

Paint the hardened base white. Mark the central point on the clock face; draw an inner circle 3½ in (9 cm) diameter, and outer circle 7 in (17 cm) diameter with a compass. Trace on to it the designs from page 119, remembering to reverse motifs for the right-hand side of the clock and paint as illustrated, or use adhesive motifs. Paint both sides of the clock face with at least two coats of varnish for added strength, and varnish the hole at the back.

Fit the hands and movement according to the manufacturer's instructions; the movement has its own triangular-shaped loop attached at the top for hanging the clock up.

Motifs for clock-face

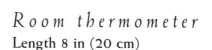

Room thermometer
Length 8 in (20 cm)

Inexpensive gauges can be found at garden centres or general household stores. Measure the length and width of the gauge, roll dough to a flat sheet, and cut a piece 1 in (2.5 cm) wider and longer than the measurements and ½ in (12 mm) deep. Depress the back of the gauge into the surface of the dough. Make a hole in the top with the blunt end of a bamboo skewer for hanging. Position the gauge on to the hardened strip and secure with glue and paint a floral design around the edge. Cut a piece of green felt to size and glue on the back to neaten.

Pretzel bun

Cottage loaf

Home-baked bread

Bread displayed in a basket with a pretty gingham cloth makes an attractive decoration for a kitchen. It is easy to achieve the rustic home-baked appearance by using real seeds and grains for the decoration. Experiment with poppy and sesame seeds or rock salt chips.

Roll dough into small buns and slightly flatten into bap shapes. Form dough into one small and one large ball. Now sit the small ball on the larger one and indent the centre with your thumb to form the bun of a cottage loaf. Plait tubes of dough together to make a braided loaf. Roll out a thick tube of dough and slash diagonally down its length to create a French stick. Twist each end of a long tube of dough around on itself, overlapping one end over the other to fashion a pretzel-shaped bun (see diagram).

Moisten the tops of the loaves and rolls with water and sprinkle on seeds or crushed rock salt. Dry the bread shapes in the oven. Using a pastry brush, paint them first with a salt-water glaze and finish with an egg glaze. When browned in the oven you can achieve a home-baked look to your pieces.

70

★ ★ ★ ★ ★ ★ ★ ★ ★

Picture frame

Measures 10 in (25 cm) x 8 in (20 cm)

Roll out the dough to a sheet of the above measurements and at least ¼ in (6 mm) thick. Cut out an oblong from the middle, leaving a 2 in (5 cm) border to the frame. Make a square of dough ½ in (12 mm) larger than the inner square for the back of the frame. Mark lines in the four corners of the frame to represent angled joints. Cut out two leaves, using the templates in the pattern section on page 116, and position them in the corner of the frame as illustrated. Shape balls of dough over the leaves for the grapes. Dry the frame and backing pieces and join the backing to the frame with dough paste or household adhesive. Remember to leave the top edge open to insert a chosen photograph. To hang the frame, fasten a linen hanging loop to the back. To make it free-standing, glue a hardened triangular strip of dough on to the back as a frame support. Paint both sides of the frame with gold poster paint.

★ ★ ★ ★ ★ ★ ★ ★ ★ ★ ★ ★ ★ ★

72

Bathing beauty

Measures 9 in (23 cm) x 10 in (25 cm)

Roll half the basic recipe to a flat sheet
¼ in (6 mm) thick, and from it cut a rectangle
5½ in (14 cm) wide x 6¾ in (17 cm) high. Curve
the top of the piece as shown in the photograph,
using a sharp knife to round off the corners.
Mould a bath shape from the dough, and secure
to the plaque with water. Roll a ball of dough for
the head, slightly flatten it between your palms
and stick to the plaque, allowing enough room
for body, leg and arm pieces. Fashion the
remainder of the figure to fit above the bath, but
to appear as though it is sitting below the rim.

Cut a semicircle approximately ½ in (12 mm)
larger than the top and width of the head; pinch
the straight edge into gathers forming the
shower cap and secure to the head with water.

Make additional features as illustrated on
pages 22–3. Two oblongs, each measuring 4 in
(10 cm) x 2½ in (6 cm), form the shutters: cut
out the heart shapes from them and mark the
wood grain with a craft knife. Place a shutter
at each side of the window opening and fix
in position with water. Use a bamboo skewer
to make a hole in the top for hanging.
Glue some pretty dried flowers into the
window-box.

★ ★ ★ ★ ★ ★ ★ ★ ★ ★ ★ ★ ★ ★ ★

Bathroom

Room name plaques

Measures 4 in (10 cm) in diameter

Roll enough dough to make a flat sheet approximately ¼ in (6 mm) thick, and from this cut out the number of 4 in (10 cm) circles that you require. The ideas given in the illustrations are for a kitchen, bathroom or toilet. Form shapes on the circles to represent the room behind the door. Make a hole in the top for hanging or use adhesive hanging loops.

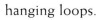

Kitchen

73

Toilet

Primrose shape

Primrose decorated basket
Height 4½ in (11.5 cm)

Grease the outside of an upturned rice-bowl with oil and secure strips of baking parchment around it. Model strips of dough over the sides. Cut a circular piece of dough to fit the base and secure in position with water. Trim dough extensions from the base of the bowl. Twist together two lengths of dough that are long enough to fit the circumference of the bowl. Join the strips into a ring and make a rim on the bowl by pressing over the edges of the strips. Dry the bowl in the oven. When hardened, use the paper extensions to ease the dough mould from the china bowl. Fashion flowers and leaves from dough and make a hole for the stamen in the middle of the flowers with the blunt end of a bamboo skewer. Secure leaves and flowers to the rim of the bowl with a dough paste and harden again in the oven. Glue a stamen into the hole of each flower after painting.

Primrose in plant pot
Height 6 in (15 cm)

Flatten a piece of dough into a plant-pot shape, cut a strip of dough for the top rim and fix in position with water. Cut eight or ten dough leaves, using the template from the pattern section on page 116, and trace the veins on each leaf with the point of a knife. Anchor the leaves to the back of the pot, curve them over the front rim and secure with water. Form flowers out of dough, using the illustrated outline to make your template or a flower cutter. Make a hole in the centre of each flower with a cocktail stick to hold the stamen. Position the flowers over the leaves in a pretty, balanced arrangement. Close up a few flowers to make them look as though they are just opening out. When hard, glue a stamen in the middle of each flower. You can make the ivy version as an alternative.

The same method can also be used to make this ivy variation

75

Country cottage

Measures 11 in (28 cm) x 10 in (25 cm)

Model the cottage from two flat sheets of dough, one shaped as the front of the house and the other as the roof. Cut the door, shutters, and window-boxes from scraps of dough. Pad the under-side of the porch roof with dough. Mark a stone pattern on the front wall with a craft knife. Fashion flowers around the door, using a small cutter to shape dough flowers.

Slash the roof with a sharp knife to reproduce thatch, marking crosses along the top about ½ in (12 mm) down to simulate straw bindings.

★   ★   ★   ★   ★   ★   ★   ★   ★   ★   ★   ★   ★   ★   ★

Mermaid mirror

Length 16 in (40 cm)

Ask your local glass shop or picture framer to cut a heart shape out of mirror glass to the measurement of the heart template in the pattern section on pages 120–1. Trace the heart outline on to a ¼ in (6 mm) thick piece of plywood, allowing ¾ in (2 cm) of wood to extend beyond the edge of the mirror outline; draw a handle shape below the heart with a pencil. Clamp the wood in a vice and cut the shape out with a hand fretsaw, working the saw in an up and down movement and keeping close to the outline. Smooth any rough edges with sandpaper. Using a glue gun, glue the mirror to the plywood at the edges only. Paint the edges of the

Shell soap-dish

4¾ in (12 cm)

Press the dough firmly around the under-side of a scallop shell. Trim excess dough away from the shell's edge. Dry the model in the oven and when firm remove the shell and harden the surface which contains the shell imprint. Paint the surface in sea colours; for example, blue, turquoise and jade, and the under-side white. Glue a bead trim carefully around the perimeter of the shell.

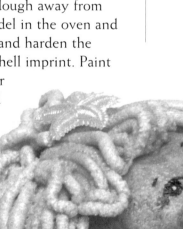

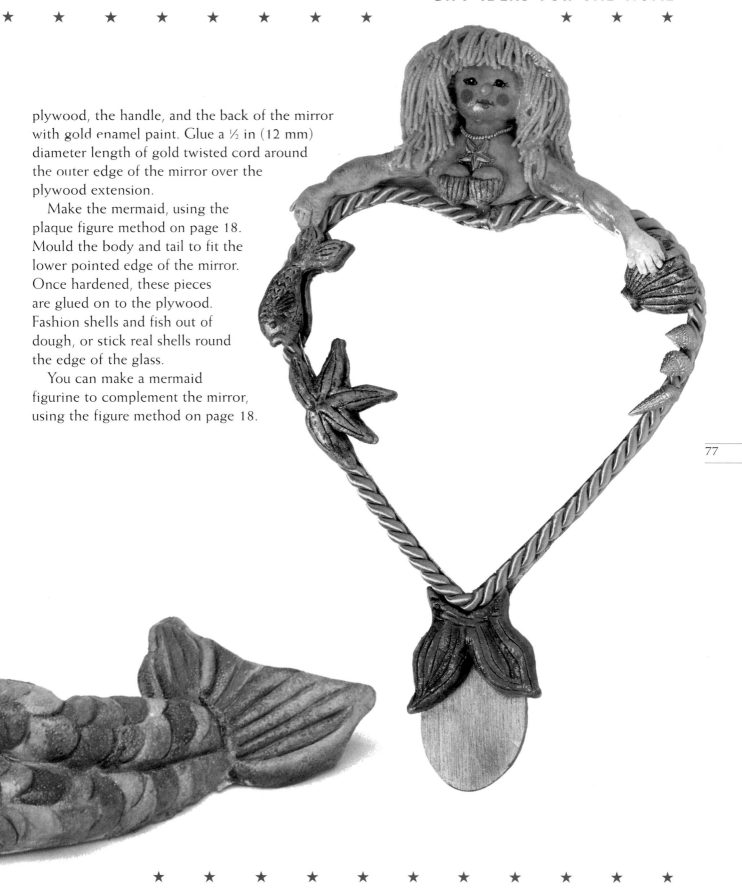

plywood, the handle, and the back of the mirror with gold enamel paint. Glue a ½ in (12 mm) diameter length of gold twisted cord around the outer edge of the mirror over the plywood extension.

Make the mermaid, using the plaque figure method on page 18. Mould the body and tail to fit the lower pointed edge of the mirror. Once hardened, these pieces are glued on to the plywood. Fashion shells and fish out of dough, or stick real shells round the edge of the glass.

You can make a mermaid figurine to complement the mirror, using the figure method on page 18.

77

Roses in a basket

Measures 12 in (30 cm) square

Make the basket following the method for weaving on page 29 and the rest of the model following the method for the poinsettia basket on page 47. Model the roses and leaves from dough tinted with food colourings. The method for making roses is given on page 28. Give the basket a salt-water and egg glaze finish to achieve a rustic look. Tie a ribbon bow around the handle of the basket.

Christmas hearth

Measures 12 in (30 cm) x 7 in (18 cm)

Roll the dough to a flat sheet of the above dimensions. Cut out strips of dough to fit the mantelpiece and the top shelf and cut out the curved mirror and ceramic tiles. Make a carriage clock from a small oblong piece of dough and fashion four tiny balls for the feet. Cut strips of dough to make the rungs of the fire grate and shape dough into small pieces of coal and logs. Mould a sitting cat shape from dough. Angle the edges of the hearth neatly with a craft knife. Assemble all the pieces as shown in the photograph. Insert a hanging loop into the back of the plaque at the top.

When the plaque is dry paint the features as illustrated or match to your own colour schemes. Finish off with gold tinsel-covered wire for the swag, a mini garland, some beads for baubles, and doll's house trims such as candlesticks and a Santa Claus figure.

CHAPTER EIGHT

Advent Ideas

Advent garland

Measures 10 in (25 cm) in diameter

Form dough tubes into a twisted garland (see pages 15–16) and make poinsettia flowers and leaves using the templates from the pattern section on page 116.

Using a petal-shaped cutter, cut four candle holders from dough ¾ in (2 cm) thick and fix to the garland with water. Place a candle in the middle of each petal to form the holding cup, and remove before drying. Arrange the leaves and petals between the holders. Make five or six tiny balls of dough for the stamens in the middle of each flower.

Santa in his sleigh

Board measures 22 in (56 cm) x 15 in (37 cm)

Use the templates on pages 124–5 to trace the outline of Santa and his reindeer on to tracing paper. Lay the tracing over a sheet of dough ¼ in (6 mm) thick and prick out the design with the point of a needle. Cut out the design with a sharp knife.

Paint the pieces as illustrated, and glue them to a hessian covered notice-board. Screw twenty-four brass rings into the frame along the base edge. Tie ribbons to the rings and attach small presents to each of them. Using adhesive numbers, randomly number the rings from one to twenty-four.

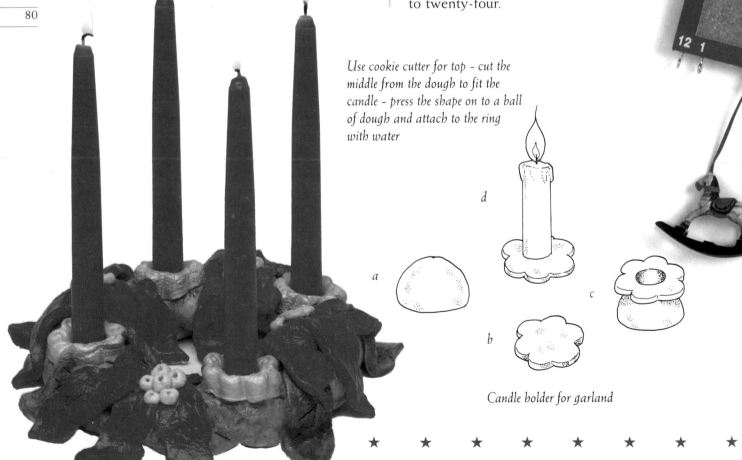

Use cookie cutter for top - cut the middle from the dough to fit the candle - press the shape on to a ball of dough and attach to the ring with water

d

a

c

b

Candle holder for garland

★ ★ ★ ★ ★ ★ ★ ★ ★

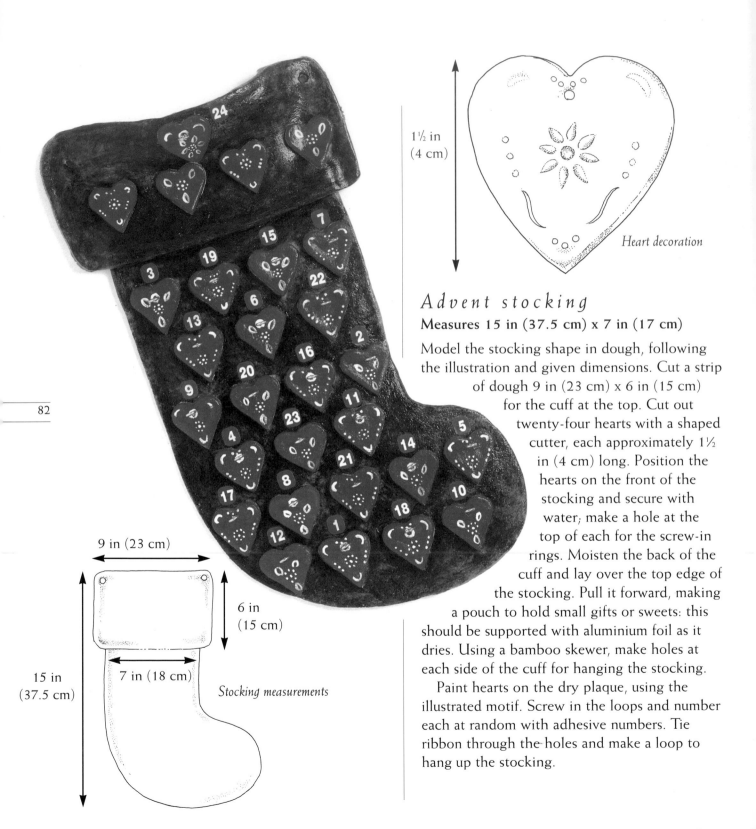

1½ in
(4 cm)

Heart decoration

Advent stocking

Measures 15 in (37.5 cm) x 7 in (17 cm)

Model the stocking shape in dough, following
the illustration and given dimensions. Cut a strip
of dough 9 in (23 cm) x 6 in (15 cm)
for the cuff at the top. Cut out
twenty-four hearts with a shaped
cutter, each approximately 1½
in (4 cm) long. Position the
hearts on the front of the
stocking and secure with
water; make a hole at the
top of each for the screw-in
rings. Moisten the back of the
cuff and lay over the top edge of
the stocking. Pull it forward, making
a pouch to hold small gifts or sweets: this
should be supported with aluminium foil as it
dries. Using a bamboo skewer, make holes at
each side of the cuff for hanging the stocking.

Paint hearts on the dry plaque, using the
illustrated motif. Screw in the loops and number
each at random with adhesive numbers. Tie
ribbon through the holes and make a loop to
hang up the stocking.

82

9 in (23 cm)

6 in
(15 cm)

15 in
(37.5 cm)

7 in (18 cm)

Stocking measurements

CHAPTER NINE

Garlands

Fruit garland
Measures 12 in (30 cm) in diameter

Uses four quantities of the basic recipe.
Make the garland in stages. First, prepare the
foundation from two plaited halves of dough
joined at each end to form a large ring. Roll
three tubes of dough for each plait; they need
to be 24 in (60 cm) long x ¾ in (2 cm) in
diameter. Plait the tubes and form them into a
joined ring. Dry the plaited ring in the oven.

Decorate the garland with pear halves,
tangerines, apples and leaves made from dough.
To shape pears, form dough into a sliced pear
silhouette, the top of the dough flat
and the under-side curved.
Insert a clove at the top for

a stem, and at the bottom for the bud tip.
Outline the centre of the pear with a knife and
embed the sunflower seeds as illustrated. Form
dough apples with cloves for stems and buds.
Make the tangerines from balls of dough and
give them a textured effect by imprinting all
over with a star nozzle. Attach the fruit to the
hardened garland with dough paste.

When the fruit is completely dry, glaze the
garland with a salt-water glaze and finish with
an egg glaze. For a rustic look, brown the high
spots under a grill. Paint both sides of the
garland with two coats of varnish. Tie a
satin ribbon at the top of the
garland, forming it into a
decorative bow.

★ ★ ★ ★ ★ ★ ★ ★ ★

Dry flower garland
Measures 10 in (25 cm) in diameter

Form two tubes of dough, approximately
18 in (45 cm) long x 1 in (2.5 cm) in
diameter. Twist them together and join
up into a ring. After hardening the
garland, glaze with salt-water and
then finish with an egg glaze.
Glue an arrangement of dried
flowers to the lower edge of the
garland. Choose festive colours of
red and green, or neutral tones
for a country look. Glue a
6 in (15 cm) long x 3 in (8 cm)
wide ribbon at the back on the top
edge of the garland. You can add a
gold dough bow on the hanging
ribbon for a dramatic effect.

★ ★ ★ ★ ★ ★ ★ ★ ★ ★ ★ ★

★ ★ ★ ★ ★ ★ ★ ★ ★ ★ ★ ★ ★ ★ ★ ★

Pasta garland

Measures 8 in (20 cm) in diameter

Model a 16 in (40 cm) x 1½ in (4 cm) diameter tube into a ring and flatten the top edge. Embed the pasta bows around the ring, each bow slightly overlapping the next one. Spray the hardened ring with gold paint. Finish off with a gold bow glued at the top. Attach an adhesive linen hook to the top on the back for hanging.

Horseshoe twist

Depth 8 in (20 cm)

Roll two tubes of dough 20 in (50 cm) long x ¾in (2 cm) in diameter. Twist the tubes together and pinch the ends. Form a horseshoe shape from the twist and place on a cookie tray. Make holes with a skewer in the ends of the horseshoe for inserting the hanging ribbon. Glue a floral Christmas decoration to the middle of the curve. Insert ribbon through the holes and tie into a long hanging loop.

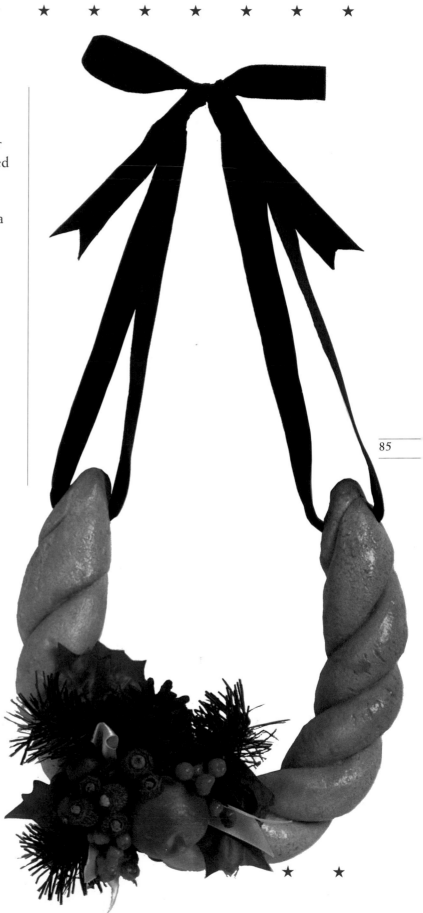

85

★ ★ ★ ★ ★ ★ ★ ★ ★

Autumn garland

Measures 10 in (25 cm) in diameter

Uses three quantities of the basic recipe.

Decorate the garland with acorns, horse-chestnuts, berries, apples and leaves made from dough; the pine cones are real.

Make the garland in stages. Attach the decorations to a hardened ring with dough paste. Form two tubes of dough, each 18 in (45 cm) long x 1 in (2.5 cm) in diameter, and twist them together. Join the twists into a ring. Paint the hardened ring in raw sienna (pigment) watercolour paint.

Method for chestnuts

*Snip dough cup
with scissors*

Horse-chestnuts

Make four dough balls approximately 1¼ in (3 cm) in diameter and harden in the oven. Cut out four circles for cups, each measuring 1¼ in (3 cm) in diameter and ¼ in (6 mm) thick. Coat the base of the balls with dough paste, mould the cups of dough around the lower halves of the balls and press firmly to secure. To form the spikes on the horse-chestnut shells, snip the surface of the dough into points with scissors.

★ ★ ★ ★ ★ ★ ★ ★ ★ ★ ★ ★ ★ ★ ★

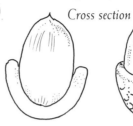

Acorns

Make eight nuts from pieces of dough measuring
¾ in (2 cm) long x ½ in (12 mm) in diameter and
round off the ends. Cut eight circles of dough
using the wide end of a nozzle as a cutter; coat
one end of each nut with paste and press a
circular dough cup around the base.

Cross section   *Indent dough cup
with end of icing
nozzle*

Apples

Roll four dough balls
measuring 2½ in (6 cm)
diameter and press a
clove into the top of each
for stalks.

87

Berries

Make eight dough balls, each measuring
¾ in (2 cm) diameter.

Leaves

Cut eight each of the oak and plain leaves, using
the templates from the pattern section on pages
116 and 117.

Assembly

Paint all the hardened components in their
appropriate colours. The apples should be
painted in two tones to suggest a ripening
appearance. Glue two oak leaves together and
fix an acorn to the top of each leaf. Attach the
nuts, leaves and fruits in a balanced arrangement
around the ring with a glue gun. Varnish the
front and back. Complete with a bow and loop
tied at the top.

★ ★ ★ ★ ★ ★ ★ ★ ★ ★ ★ ★ ★ ★ ★

Holly garland

Measures 8 in (20 cm) in diameter

Make the foundation from a twisted heart or
circle shape of dough. Use icing cutters to shape
the holly leaves, and roll dough into small balls
for the berries. Insert half a paper-clip for
hanging. Finish off the hardened garland by
tying a big tartan or satin ribbon bow at the top.

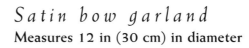

Satin bow garland
Measures 12 in (30 cm) in diameter

Use two quantities of the basic recipe for this garland. With any left-over dough you can make small bows; these are ideal to make into picture hook decorations or name place settings. Roll out the dough to a ¼ in (6 mm) thickness on a flour dusted work-top. Cut twelve equal lengths from the rolled dough measuring 8 in (20 cm) x 3¼ in (8 cm). Six lengths form the bow ties and six the bows.

To make one bow use two lengths of dough. Cut a V from the narrow ends of one length. Roll two tubes of dough each measuring 3 in (7.5 cm) long x ¾ in (2 cm) in diameter from the left-over dough for padding the bow. Lay these tubes 2 in (5 cm) in at each end of the second length. Take the ends of this strip and roll them over the padding to the middle, fixing down with some water. Moisten the back of the bow and lay it over the tie, pinching the middle slightly to form a waist. Make the knot in the centre of the bow from an oval piece of dough approximately 2¾ in (7 cm) long x 1½ in (4 cm) in diameter. Lay this piece over the middle and fix at the back with water. To complete the effect of a knotted bow, mark the gathers with the blunt end of a barbecue stick. The garland is made by laying the ties of one bow over the other, linking the six into a circle. Carefully slide the garland on to a lined cookie sheet and dry in the oven. If the garland is to be hung, add a string loop at the back before drying. Paint the bows red when dry, highlighting with white to resemble satin bows. Varnish when dry.

89

Rustic Crete garland
Measures 8 in (20 cm) in diameter

Decorate a ring of dough with leaves and
flowers imprinted with the large teeth of a comb
(see diagram). Secure a string hanging loop to
the back of the ring with small balls of dough.
Harden the garland, then finish with a salt-
water glaze and egg glaze. Decorate with a
brown satin bow tied at the top.

*Cut circle in half
and shape leaf*

*Indent dough with
teeth on a comb*

*Indent scallop edge
with comb*

*Insert
peppercorn*

90

CHAPTER TEN

Tree Decorations

There are many different ideas that lend themselves to creating excellent tree decorations; the following give you a base from which to work. Keep the colours to a particular colour theme, such as red and white, all gold, gold and white, and so on. In subsequent years, make the decorations in new colours to ring the changes.

Toy town shapes

Trace the shapes from the pattern section on pages 116 and 117 on to patchwork plastic or stiff card and cut out templates for each. Lay the cut shape on the rolled dough, pressing it in slightly, and carve around the outline with a sharp knife. Add extra details at this stage, such as buttons or medals; remember to make a small hole in each for the hanging cord.

Design your own templates on patchwork plastic.

91

Cookie cut decorations

Roll the dough to ¼ in (6 mm) thick and use a
variety of shaped cutters to produce simple
and effective decorations. Make embellished
shapes as illustrated, or press seeds, pods,
and so on into the dough to form patterns.
Glaze the background before drying, or
paint it after hardening. You can paint
your shapes with a white base and then
paint gold patterns on them to make
innovative decorations.

Three-dimensional shapes

Again, use cookie cutters for the foundation
of each shape. Make the patterns with small
cutters or canapé cutters. Use the wide end of
a piping nozzle to remove the centres of the
small shapes. Moisten these with water and
stick a smaller shape over a larger one to create
a three-dimensional effect. After drying, paint
with your chosen colour theme. Miniature
braids, twists and garlands make attractive tree
decorations; additional ribbons or dried
flowers can be glued on after the
varnishing process.

Christmas angel

Height 8 in (20 cm)

Make a chubby girl figure dressed in a long dough gown using the flat figure method on pages 18–19. Use a large heart-shaped cutter to cut a heart from rolled dough and snip it down the centre to form the wings. The angel is holding a candle (a cake candle is suitable for this purpose). Imprint the hands to make a hollow so you can glue it in position after drying. Attach a paper-clip hanging loop to the back of the figure. For the halo, form tinsel-covered wire into an oval and glue it to the back of the angel's head.

Christmas fairy

Height 9 in (23 cm)

Create a female figure with the legs and arms attached, using the method described on page 22. Shape the feet into pointed ballet shoes and indent one hand with a cocktail stick to enable it to hold the wand. Attach small balls of dough for the breasts and give the figure long straight hair. Insert a paper-clip hanging loop into the top.

For the dress, fold a piece of white netting 24 in (60 cm) long x 12 in (30 cm) wide in half and run a gathering thread through the fold. Draw the net skirt up and secure around the waist by knotting the thread at the back. Cut a piece of white fabric to cover the visible body section under the breasts, and glue into place. Make a bra from a strip of scallop-edged lace; two scallops form the bra cups. Glue over the breasts, and fix strips of ribbon for bra straps.

For the crown, join a 4½ in (11 cm) length of metallic lace to form a ring and glue the overlapping ends. Glue the base of the crown to the head.

For the wings, bend two gold chenille-covered wires into wing shapes, twist the ends together and glue to the back of the figure.

To complete the Christmas fairy, glue gold stars on to the dress and a large star-shaped sequin to a cocktail stick for the wand. Secure the wand to the hand with glue.

You could also make the fairy into a wall plaque by gluing it on to a piece of wood.

★ ★ ★ ★ ★ ★ ★ ★ ★

★ ★ ★ ★ ★ ★ ★ ★ ★ ★ ★ ★ ★ ★ ★ ★

CHAPTER ELEVEN

Nativity

It is best to make the figures in stages, using a hardened shape to support the weight of the gowns and headdresses. For method see pages 22–3.

Mary

Height 5 in (12 cm)

Use a 3½ in (9 cm) high L-shaped mould as the foundation for the kneeling figures.

For the body, roll an oblong piece of dough measuring 12 in (30 cm) x 6 in (15 cm). Pleat the dough around the top of the body and tuck under the knees, securing with dough paste. Knot a cord tassel at the waist. For the head, model a dough ball measuring 1½ in (4 cm), position it on the end of a cocktail stick and secure with dough paste. Add hair and features as illustrated.

Dress the arms by wrapping triangular shapes of dough around the tubes, pressing the edges together with water to secure. Bend the arms and press one on to the body at each shoulder. Model two hands from balls of dough, attaching each at the end of the arms in a praying position. Paint Mary's eyes looking downwards, to appear as though in prayer.

Joseph

Height 6 in (15 cm)

Model Joseph in the same way as Mary and add a beard and a long nose. For the cloak, drape and pleat an oblong of dough around the shoulders.

Paint a striped pattern on Joseph's gown to simulate coarsely woven fabric. Draw the eyes so that they appear to look towards the baby, giving Joseph a loving, paternal air.

Baby Jesus

Length 3½ in (9 cm)

Model the head and body shape to the length given above. Cut a ½ in (12 mm) wide length of dough for the swaddling cloth and wrap it around the head and body, similar to an Egyptian mummy.

Sheep and lamb

Width of sheep 3¼ in (8 cm); width of lamb 2 in (5 cm)

Model the sheep on a straight mould. Fashion the head from a ball of dough. Pinch the nose into shape and mark the mouth by slitting the dough with a knife. Press some dough through a fine sieve to reproduce the sheep's wool coat and attach to the body. Shape the lamb from a small ball of dough for the head, and a larger piece for the body. Secure an ear to each side of the head and join the head to the body with water. Cast the model as though curled up asleep.

★ ★ ★ ★ ★

The barn

Measures 18 in (45 cm) x 14in (35cm)

Make the barn from two wooden fruit crates; your local fruit and vegetable stall will let you have some free of charge. Lay one crate on its side. Cut an apex roof shape from the side of the second crate and glue or staple it to the back of the first crate. Paint the wood inside and out with a medium oak wood stain. Wire two wicker frames together to make the barn roof, and sit this on the apex support (these frames can be purchased from flower shops or garden centres). You may need wooden chocks to act as supports to each side on the front edge.

Line the floor with hay and display nativity figures in it. Wire pieces of twig together to make the ladder.

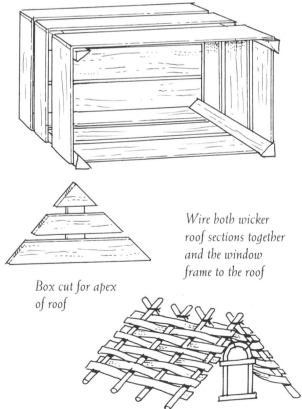

Fruit crate

Box cut for apex of roof

Wire both wicker roof sections together and the window frame to the roof

The Three Kings

Height 7 in (18 cm)

Model the three figures as for Mary. Each king wears a cloak and carries a gift. Use painted glass beads to decorate the dough caskets. Each figure has a dough candle holder fixed to its head. Use cake candles in the holders.

When the figures have hardened, decorate the robes by painting them in rich patterns such as the gold fleur-de-lis illustrated, or stick on sequin shapes after varnishing.

CHAPTER TWELVE

Table Decorations

Centre-piece for the Christmas dinner table

Measures 10 in (25 cm) in diameter

A twisted dough garland forms the base (for method see pages 15–16). Cut four star shapes from thickly rolled dough; they need to be at least ¾ in (2 cm) deep to support the candles. Space the star holders evenly around the top of the garland and moisten with water to secure. Press a candle into each star to imprint the shape of the holding cups.

Spray the hardened garland with gold paint and allow to dry. Decorate the ring by wiring on artificial sprigs of pine needles and nuts. Grouped floral sprays can be purchased from department stores or garden centres: the wired stems make it easier for you to fix them to the garland. A glue gun is also ideal for securing trims. Complete the decoration by adding white roses and candles. For added safety, secure the candles in the base of the holders with adhesive putty.

★ ★ ★ ★ ★ ★ ★ ★ ★ ★ ★ ★ ★ ★

ht light holder

*...s of baking parchment are
...over an upturned rice bowl
...re the dough is shaped
...nd it.*

*Cut out heart shapes
from around edge of
bowl*

Night-light
Height 4½ in (11 cm)

Roll dough into a ¼ in (6 mm) thick circle,
larger than the bowl to be covered. Lay strips
of baking parchment over an upturned rice
bowl, extending the parchment beyond the top
and bottom edges. Fold the extensions over
each other at the top, holding in position with
water. Gently lift the rolled dough over the
bowl, and press it around the bowl. Trim excess
dough from the base with a knife. Use a heart-
shaped cutter to cut out hearts from the dough
round the sides of the bowl. Using a fish slice,
lift the mould on to a cookie sheet. When hard,
ease the shape off the mould; it helps if you
lift the dough away from the sides of the
bowl with a blunt knife.
Paint the holder with the
design illustrated, or glue
on Victorian-style scraps
before varnishing.

101

Mini apple candle holder
Height 2½ in (6 cm)

Roll five balls of dough approximately
¾ in (2 cm) diameter and press them
together to form a ring. Insert a clove in the top
of each ball for the stem. Insert a candle into
the ring to ensure that it is large enough to hold
the candle and remove before drying the ring in
the oven.

★ ★ ★ ★ ★ ★ ★ ★ ★ ★ ★

Menu holder

Measures 9 in (23 cm) x 8 in (20 cm)

Cut a rectangular sheet of dough to the above measurements from dough combined with wallpaper glue. Twist strips of dough ½ in (12 mm) wide around the border, securing them with water. Decorate the board with clusters of holly and berries made from dough. You can either make a hole in the top for hanging up the menu or a dough support to stand the menu upright on the table. Paint the board with enamel gold paint and the holly and berries in their appropriate colours. Decorate a paper insert to fit the board, write or type your Christmas menu on it and fix to the board with double sided adhesive tape.

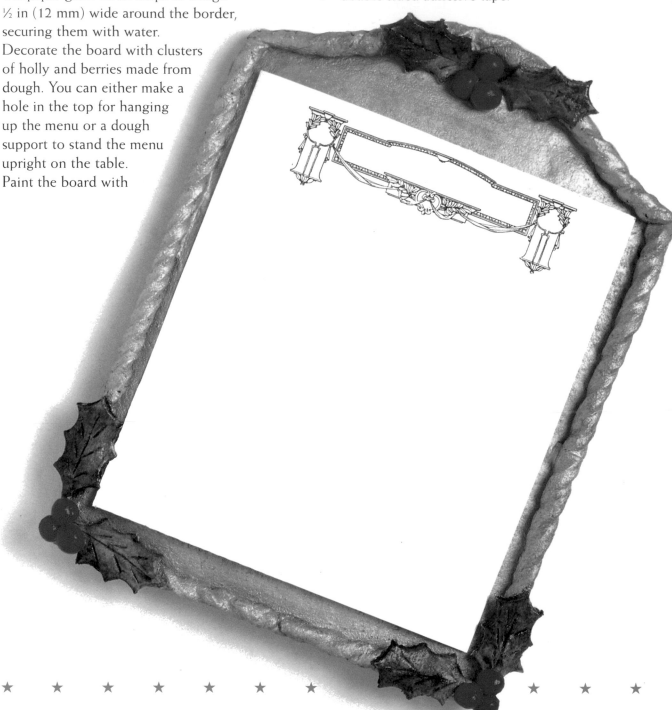

Bread basket

Measures 10 in (25 cm) in diameter

Lightly coat the exterior of an oval shaped oven-proof dish with cooking oil. Cut baking parchment into ½ in (12 mm) wide strips and position around the sides of the upturned dish. Make an oval piece of parchment to cover the base of the dish. Shape a piece of dough to fit the base and place it over the lining. Use strips of dough ½ in (12 mm) wide x ¼ in (6 mm) thick to surround the sides of the dish, securing their ends to the oval base with water. Trim the top extensions flush with the edge. Make a twist of dough ¾ in (2 cm) thick and long enough to go around the top edge. Attach with water over the cut ends, gently pressing in position. When hard, carefully ease the shape from the mould with a spatula and then remove the baking parchment lining.

The basket looks equally good painted as with a rustic glazed coating. Decorate the top edge with real ivy or make dough leaves with an ivy-shaped cutter.

Cherub candle holder

Height 4 in (10 cm)

Make a chubby reclining figure from dough using the method on pages 18–19 for the body. Cover the base of a purchased candle holder with dough. Assemble the figure at the base of the holder and position the hands to appear as though they are supporting the holder. Model the wings from two triangular pieces of dough and attach to the back of the cherub. Use a trumpet tree decoration for the trim. Twist a piece of gold tinsel wire into a halo shape and glue to the back of the cherub's head.

103

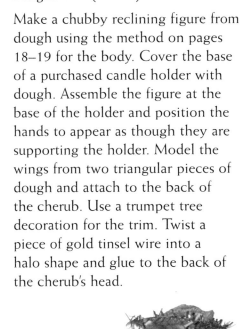

104

Cookie-shaped candle holder

Width 4 in (10 cm)

Use a small and large cutter of the same shape to make these holders. Bond the smaller dough shape to the larger with water. Use the base of a candle to imprint the centre of the smaller shape to gauge the hole size.

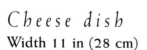

Cheese dish

Width 11 in (28 cm)

Use a shaped oven-proof dish for the mould (for example, one in the form of a leaf). Oil the exterior of the dish, then lay a ¼ in (6 mm) thick sheet of dough over it. Press the dough to the sides of the dish and cut around the outline with a sharp knife to remove the overhang. Decorate the hardened dish with vine leaves and grapes, using the motifs on page 119. Complete with a salt-water and egg glaze.

Place name setting

Measures 4 in (10 cm) x 1¾ in (4.5 cm)

Shape an oblong piece of dough to fit over a piece of stiff card folded to the above measurements. When dry, paint a festive pattern around the border, for example, the tartan design illustrated. The name of each guest is written on the card with a black or gold felt-tip pen. To re-use the setting, stick a self-adhesive label over the previous name.

105

bamboo cocktail stick

Hors-d'oeuvre sticks

Height 4 in (10 cm)

Fashion heads from dough to resemble members of your family or friends and insert a fork-shaped bamboo cocktail stick into the base of the head. Glue a piece of felt cut to size to the back of the head to neaten it.

Gingerbread cottage

Measures 8½ in (21.5 cm) x 8 in (20 cm)

Not as difficult as it looks! The easiest way to make this delightful cottage is in stages. You will need four times the basic quantity of dough, strengthened with wallpaper glue. Cut templates from card for all the components of the cottage and base, following the measurements given in the diagram.

Cut out a large, irregular, oval sheet of dough at least ½ in (12 mm) thick to the measurements given for the base. The cottage is assembled on the base once it has hardened.

Trace around the templates on to baking parchment. Roll long tubes of dough ½ in (12 mm) in diameter and layer the tubes one above the other over each traced shape. Trim the dough away at the ends where it extends beyond the outline. Bond all the tubes with water. Cut an opening for the windows and the doorway with a craft knife. Roll small tubes to make the window panels and fit them to the frame surround.

Decoration

Make the gingerbread children from scraps of dough using a tiny gingerbread figure cutter. Cut a small heart for the door plaque and two scalloped eaves to fit the short edges of the roof and add decoration. Roll a piece of dough into a block 1½ in (4 cm) x 1 in (2.5 cm) for the chimney. Slice a V shape out of the lower section to allow it to sit firmly on the sloping roof. Shape a number of flattened dough balls into irregular ovals for the paving stones.

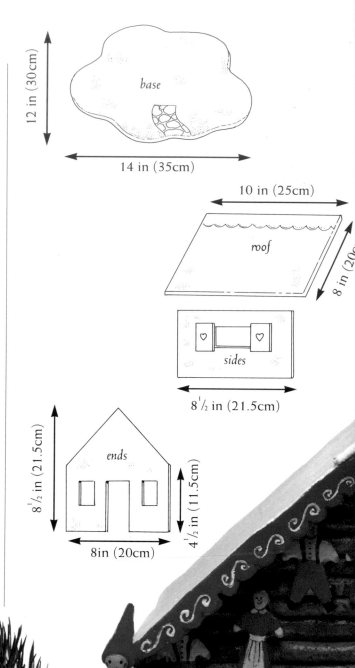

Assemble all the hardened pieces with dough paste. Join the ends and sides together, glue the walls to the base, and the middle section of the roof together. Then glue the roof on to the top edge of the walls. You may need to strengthen the roof and corners of the walls; to do this, attach supporting lengths of dough into the corners on the inside of the cottage. Glue the scalloped pieces on to the front end of the roof, and conceal the join down the middle of the roof with a strip of folded dough. Attach all the other decorations, the paving stones and the chimney as in the photograph. Dry the assembled cottage in the oven. It is possible to use a glue gun for assembling the cottage, but you will not be able to put it in the oven to dry additional soft pieces.

107

Fix the cottage to the base with glue and surround the cottage with piles of dough snow. Make a fence to go in the left-hand corner from long and short lengths of dough; mark a wood grain on them with a pointed knife.

Use purchased trims such as a Christmas tree and artificial foliage to complete the scene. The more adventurous can even make the characters from *Hansel and Gretel*.

Fir-tree

Height 6 in (5 cm)

Roll some dough into a cone shape and sit it on a base of dough cut with a petal-shaped cutter. Snip into the cone with scissors using the same method as for the owl on page 61 to form the stylized branches. Add a small Christmas elf trim or similar to complete the model.

Fir tree base

Snip dough with scissors for branches

Fir tree

Bottle jacket

Height 6 in (15 cm)

Form the waistcoat from a piece of dough over an empty wine bottle that has been oiled. Use the template on page 123 to make the pattern. After varnishing, glue ribbon ties to the back and a ribbon loop at the neck.

CHAPTER THIRTEEN

Plaques

Making friends

Measures 10 in (25 cm) x 9 in (23 cm)

Roll dough into a flat sheet and make an indented oval shape for the base. Model the snowman in the centre, with the children each side.

Paint the knitted pattern detailing onto the jumpers, hats and gloves of the children to make the figures more realistic and to add a cosiness to the scene. Glue a small pom-pom on top of each hat after varnishing the plaque. Attach a linen loop to the reverse for hanging.

Commemorative year plaque
Measures 6 in (15 cm) x 6 ¼ in (16 cm)

Use a large heart-shaped cookie cutter or mould
the dough over an oven-proof plate for the
foundation of the plaque. Decorate with letters
and numbers made from shaped cutters and
glue on Victorian scraps. Christmas wrapping
paper provides you with an alternate source
for cut-outs.

110

Santa plaque

Measures 10 in (25.5 cm) x 8in (20 cm)

Model the body without arms, and the roof-top, and lay on the card base. Embed the frame into the soft dough. Make Santa's arms and attach them to the body so that one rests on top of the ladder and the other hand holds the bottle. Model a moon shape. Harden the framed plaque and moon shape in the oven. When the model has cooled, cover the card with dark blue paper and glue it behind the model in the frame. Glue on the moon and stars as illustrated. Fasten the bottle in Santa's hands. Miniature bottles can be purchased from doll's house suppliers. Using the plaque figure method, you can make a Santa plaque on a dough base as illustrated on page 13.

A partridge in a pear tree

Twelve days of Christmas plaques
Measures 9 in (23 cm) in diameter

The best recipe to use is the one which incorporates wallpaper paste, as it is stronger. Roll dough out to a 10 in (25 cm) circle and about ½ in (12 mm) thick. Use a scalloped flan ring to cut the plaque base. Three times the basic quantity of dough is enough to make the twelve bases. Make a hole in the top of each for a hanging ribbon. Using the illustrations of each of the twelve days as a guide, make the models three-dimensional or paint the appropriate design on the twelve hardened bases.

Two turtle doves

Three French hens

★ ★ ★ ★ ★ ★ ★ ★ ★ ★

Four collie birds

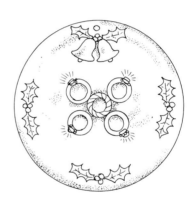

Five gold rings

Six geese a laying

★ ★ ★ ★ ★ ★ ★

★ ★ ★ ★ ★ ★ ★ ★ ★ ★

Seven swans a swimming

114

Eight maids a milking

Nine drummers drumming

★ ★ ★ ★ ★ ★ ★ ★ ★ ★

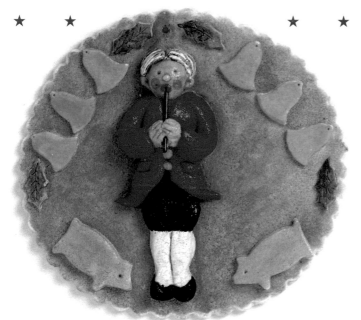

Ten pipers piping

Eleven ladies dancing

Twelve lords a leaping

CHAPTER FOURTEEN

Patterns

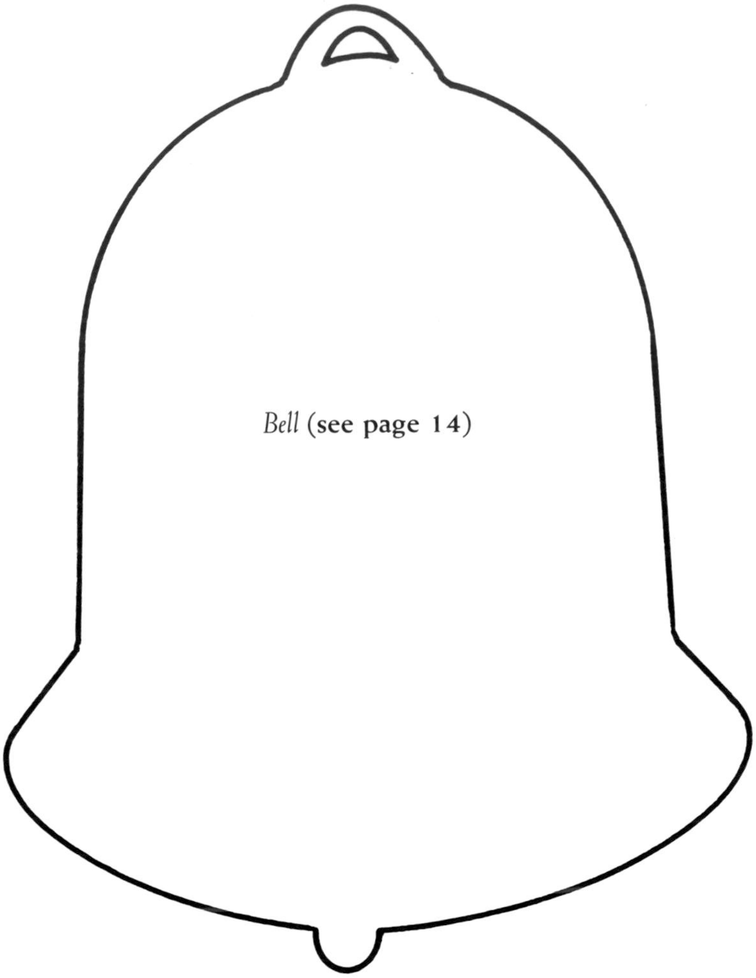

Bell (**see page 14**)

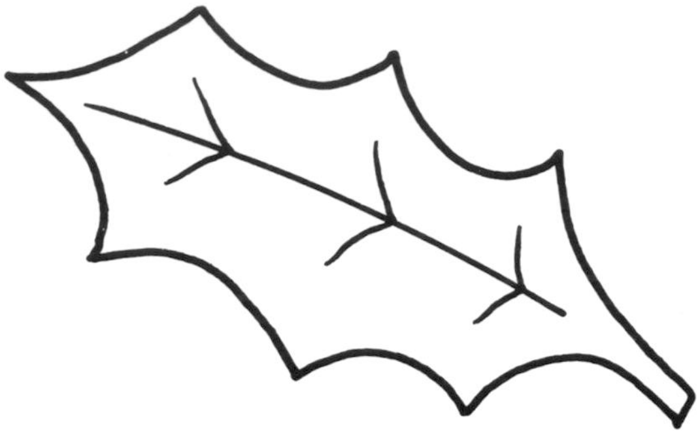

Holly (**see page 102**)

Leaf (**see page 87**)

Primrose (**see pages 28 and 74**)

Poinsettia leaf (**see page 80**)

The patterns shown here and on the following pages are the same size as the finished projects.

Rocking horse (see page 91)

Leaf (see page 87)

Drum (see page 91)

Toy soldier
(see pages 53 and 91)

Oak leaf (see page 87)

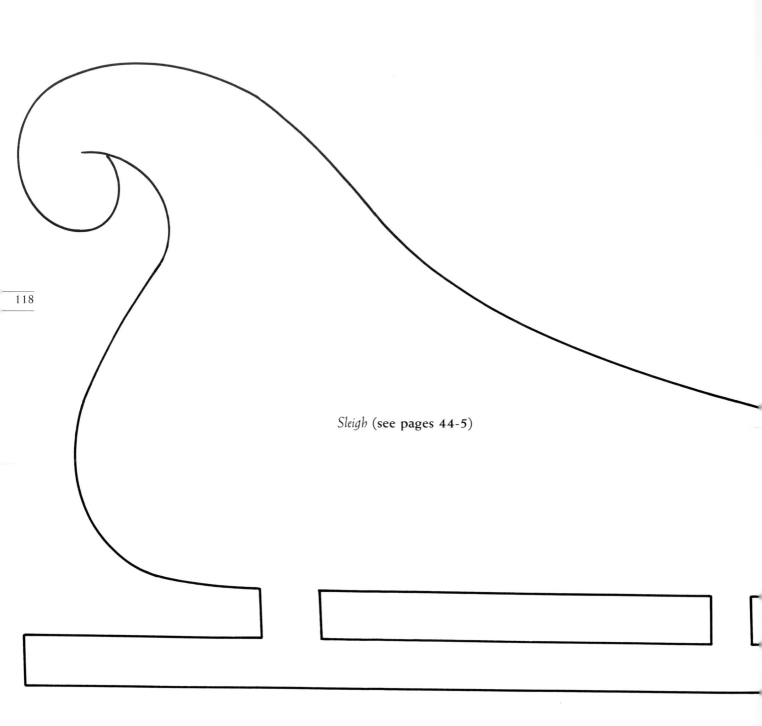

Sleigh (**see pages 44-5**)

Snowman (**see page 91**)

Motifs for clock face (**see pages 68-9**)

Babushka doll (**see page 57**)

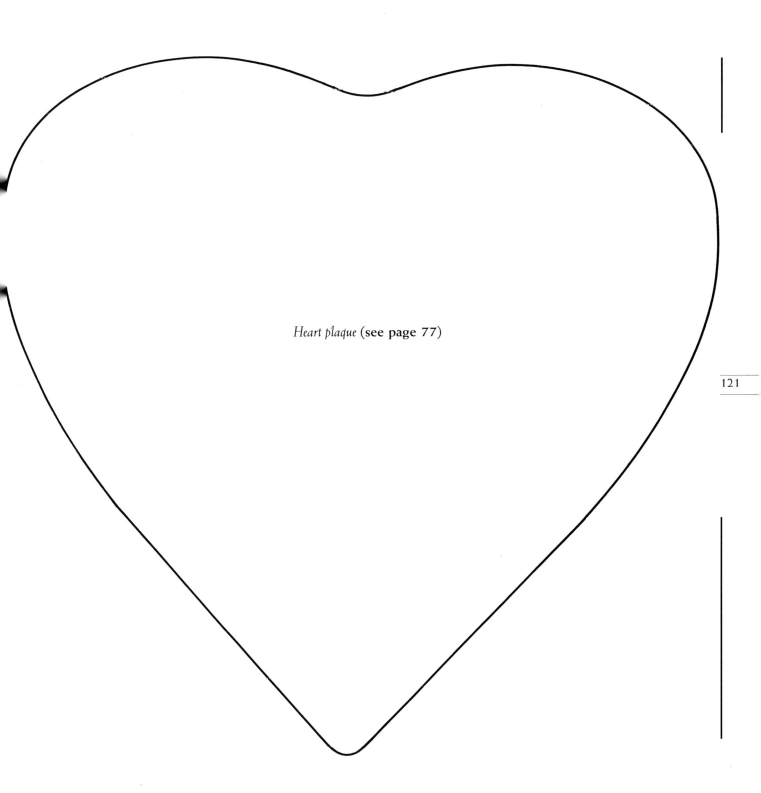

Heart plaque (**see page 77**)

121

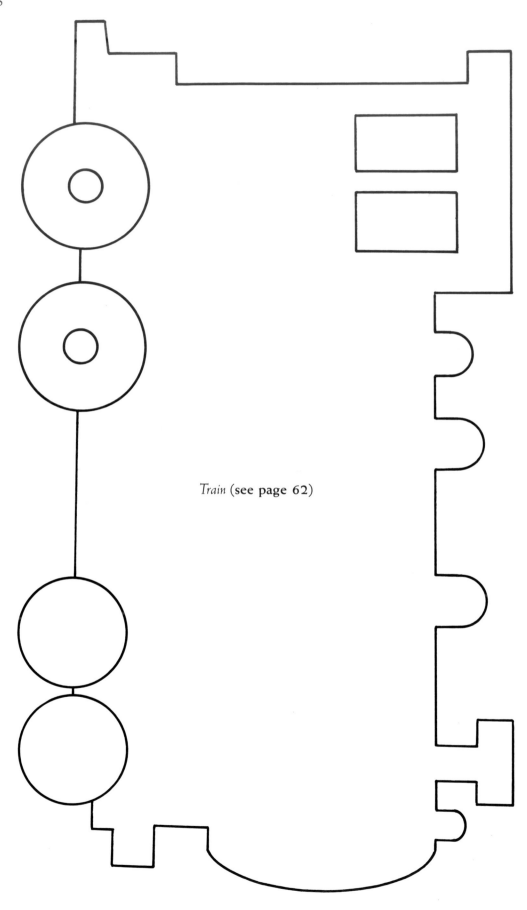

Train (**see page 62**)

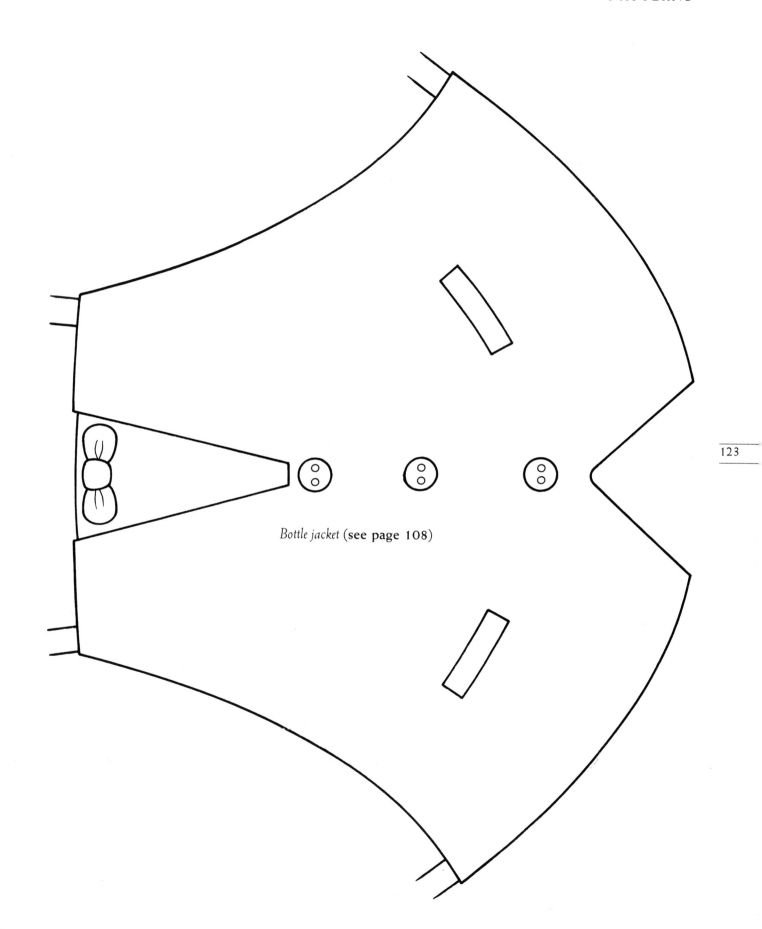

Bottle jacket (**see page** 108)

Santa and his reindeer: Advent calendar and wall hanging (**see page 81**)

Santa and his reindeer: Advent calendar and
wall hanging (**see page 81**)

125

Index

126